Introduction to JavaScript Object Notation

A To-the-Point Guide to JSON

Lindsay Bassett

Beijing · Boston · Farnham · Sebastopol · Tokyo   

Introduction to JavaScript Object Notation

by Lindsay Bassett

Published by O'Reilly Media, Inc., 1005 Gravenstein Highway North, Sebastopol, CA 95472.

O'Reilly books may be purchased for educational, business, or sales promotional use. Online editions are also available for most titles (*http://safaribooksonline.com*). For more information, contact our corporate/institutional sales department: 800-998-9938 or corporate@oreilly.com.

Editor: Meg Foley	**Indexer:** Ellen Troutman
Production Editor: Kristen Brown	**Interior Designer:** David Futato
Copyeditor: Jasmine Kwityn	**Cover Designer:** Karen Montgomery
Proofreader: Charles Roumeliotis	**Illustrator:** Rebecca Demarest

August 2015:   First Edition

Revision History for the First Edition
2015-08-04:   First Release

See *http://oreilly.com/catalog/errata.csp?isbn=9781491929483* for release details.

978-1-491-92948-3

[LSI]

Table of Contents

Preface

One thing I've learned during my journey as a web developer is that no matter how devoted I am to its subjects in spirit, finding time for said devotion is another matter. The rapidly evolving world of technology is not concerned about how busy anyone is. It does not say, "Relax, take your time to study, I understand you have a family and quiet time for studying is difficult to come by." What it says is, "Keep evolving, or become obsolete."

I wrote this book with that sentiment in mind. This book is slim—it intentionally avoids subjects like "the history of JSON."

Although I am grateful to Douglas Crockford for discovering JSON, I make no mention of him or the years during which JSON evolved into what it is today. This book is about *what it is today*. If you want to read about this history of JSON, Wikipedia has an excellent summary (*https://en.wikipedia.org/wiki/JSON#History*).

This book aims to shoot for the very heart of the subject of JSON. It is about getting to the point and getting you started quickly. It is for the busy IT professional.

Audience

As I wrote this book for the busy IT professional, I also thought quite a bit about who you are. You could be a beginning frontend web developer. Or perhaps you've been focused on server-side web application development for years, and now you need to learn JSON for a web API. You could be a PHP, Ruby, C, Java, or ASP.NET developer. That list goes on. A lot of different people in different roles want and need to learn JSON.

In this book, I avoid excessive jargon and explain prerequisite concepts for those new to web programming. I try to speak to all of you. However, I must make a few assumptions about what knowledge you already have. If you are new to web development, this should not be the very first book you pick up.

I assume you have at least a basic understanding of:

HTML
> You understand the purpose of HTML and can recognize the structure and at least a few of the tags of an HTML document.

JavaScript
> You understand the purpose of JavaScript and know what a `<script>` tag, function, and variable are. It's OK if you are only a beginner. I keep my code examples simple.

Programming concepts
> I will provide some quick explanations for concepts like object and array, for those who are new and may need a refresher. However, if you have not yet worked with *any* programming language, this book is not the place to begin.

Approach to JSON

Countless times over the years I've needed to learn new technologies, often during a project with a deadline. I buy big books, wade through tutorials, and try to absorb enough information to know what I'm doing. While I'm wading through hundreds of pages, I'm looking for the answers to these three basic questions:

- What is it?
- How can I use it?
- How can the bad guys use it?

When I wrote this book, I sought to get to the point with these questions, so you don't have to wade through to find the answers.

In Chapters 1–4, we will explore JSON at a low level. First, I will answer the ultimate question of "What is it?" From there, we will look at syntax, syntax validation, data types, and schema validation.

In Chapter 5, we will take a look at the important subject of security concerns. This chapter includes a primer on client-side and server-side concepts that are important to the remainder of the book. This chapter will answer the question of "How can the bad guys use it?"

The remaining chapters examine the many roles that JSON plays as a data interchange format. These chapters aim to answer the question, "How can I use it?"

These chapters include many examples of JSON, and technologies interacting with JSON. Some important things to note about Chapters 6–9:

Technologies

I cover several technologies, such as jQuery, AngularJS, and CouchDB, at a high level. Each of these subjects are large enough that an entire book can (and has) been written about them. I intentionally leave out installation instructions and deeper explanations about the technologies themselves. The point is to expose you to *how* these technologies are using JSON.

If you want to try out the examples shown for these technologies, you'll need to do some legwork to set everything up. However, the examples are simple. If you get things up and running at a basic level, you should be able to give them a whirl.

Code examples

You will see many code examples in this book, some in programming languages that might be new to you. The syntax will not be explained for these languages. Do not be alarmed if you don't understand the syntax. The point is for you to "get the gist" of what the code is doing, and the explanation of what the code is doing shall be provided

All of the code examples used in this book are available on this book's GitHub repository (*https://github.com/lindsaybassett/json*).

The ultimate point of Chapters 6–9 is to expose you to how JSON is being used out in the world today, and to get your idea wheels spinning for your own projects. If you never saw JSON being used as a document in a document store database, would you think to use it in a project? Knowing is half the battle.

In each chapter, a balance is sought between getting to the point and giving you enough information so that you are not left with any major holes in your education. Ultimately, the entire book is structured to get you up and running with JSON quickly, without sacrificing the deeper understanding of what JSON is and the purposes it may serve.

Conventions Used in This Book

The following typographical conventions are used in this book:

Italic

Indicates new terms, URLs, email addresses, filenames, and file extensions.

`Constant width`

Used for program listings, as well as within paragraphs to refer to program elements such as variable or function names, databases, data types, environment variables, statements, and keywords.

Constant width bold
> Shows commands or other text that should be typed literally by the user.

Constant width italic
> Shows text that should be replaced with user-supplied values or by values determined by context.

This element signifies a tip or suggestion.

This element signifies a general note.

This element indicates a warning or caution.

Using Code Examples

Supplemental material (code examples, exercises, etc.) is available for download at *https://github.com/lindsaybassett/json*.

This book is here to help you get your job done. In general, if example code is offered with this book, you may use it in your programs and documentation. You do not need to contact us for permission unless you're reproducing a significant portion of the code. For example, writing a program that uses several chunks of code from this book does not require permission. Selling or distributing a CD-ROM of examples from O'Reilly books does require permission. Answering a question by citing this book and quoting example code does not require permission. Incorporating a significant amount of example code from this book into your product's documentation does require permission.

We appreciate, but do not require, attribution. An attribution usually includes the title, author, publisher, and ISBN. For example: "*Introduction to JavaScript Object Notation* by Lindsay Bassett (O'Reilly). Copyright 2015 Lindsay Bassett, 978-1-491-92948-3."

If you feel your use of code examples falls outside fair use or the permission given above, feel free to contact us at *permissions@oreilly.com*.

Safari® Books Online

 *Safari Books Online* is an on-demand digital library that delivers expert content in both book and video form from the world's leading authors in technology and business.

Technology professionals, software developers, web designers, and business and creative professionals use Safari Books Online as their primary resource for research, problem solving, learning, and certification training.

Safari Books Online offers a range of plans and pricing for enterprise, government, education, and individuals.

Members have access to thousands of books, training videos, and prepublication manuscripts in one fully searchable database from publishers like O'Reilly Media, Prentice Hall Professional, Addison-Wesley Professional, Microsoft Press, Sams, Que, Peachpit Press, Focal Press, Cisco Press, John Wiley & Sons, Syngress, Morgan Kaufmann, IBM Redbooks, Packt, Adobe Press, FT Press, Apress, Manning, New Riders, McGraw-Hill, Jones & Bartlett, Course Technology, and hundreds more. For more information about Safari Books Online, please visit us online.

How to Contact Us

Please address comments and questions concerning this book to the publisher:

O'Reilly Media, Inc.
1005 Gravenstein Highway North
Sebastopol, CA 95472
800-998-9938 (in the United States or Canada)
707-829-0515 (international or local)
707-829-0104 (fax)

We have a web page for this book, where we list errata, examples, and any additional information. You can access this page at *http://bit.ly/intro_JS_object_notation*.

To comment or ask technical questions about this book, send email to *bookquestions@oreilly.com*.

For more information about our books, courses, conferences, and news, see our website at *http://www.oreilly.com*.

Find us on Facebook: *http://facebook.com/oreilly*

Follow us on Twitter: *http://twitter.com/oreillymedia*

Watch us on YouTube: *http://www.youtube.com/oreillymedia*

Acknowledgments

First off, I'd like to thank my husband, Rhett, for his encouragement and support in all of my writing endeavors, and for being understanding on all of those days where I was hiding in the dark hunched over my laptop.

I'd also like to thank Douglas Crockford for creating JSON and giving me something fun to write about. I'm so grateful to my technical reviewers, Shelley Powers and Tom Marrs, for their constructive feedback that helped evolve this book. Any errors are my own.

My editor, Meg Foley, was an absolute joy to work with.

Finally, I'd like to thank O'Reilly for giving my book a home and releasing it into the wild. I've always been a big fan of O'Reilly books, and after working with O'Reilly this year, I'm an even bigger fan.

CHAPTER 1

What Is JSON?

Before we look at JSON from a low-level point of view, let's take a look at JSON from about 6,000 feet. From the mountain summit, we can see JSON flitting about in the world, carrying data in its lightweight format. If we look through our binoculars at JSON, we will see data among many curly bracket characters ({}). However, if we step back, and watch *how* it's being used, we will ultimately see that it is a data interchange format.

JSON Is a Data Interchange Format

A data interchange format is a text format used to exchange data between platforms. Another data interchange format you may already have heard of is XML. The world needs data interchange formats, like XML and JSON, to exchange data between very different systems.

Imagine for a moment a world comprised of hundreds of tiny, isolated islands among a vast ocean. Each island has its own unique language and customs. The islands all have seafaring merchants that travel long distances between the islands. Outside trade is an integral part of all the island economies and contributes to a high standard of living for the islanders. If it weren't for the highly trained carrier seagulls, this would not be possible.

The carrier seagulls move from island to island, carrying a paper report of data on which goods are in the highest demand. This way, merchants find out where they should move to next, and which goods they should acquire before embarking on their long voyages across the oceans. This important data allows all the islands to prosper without the threat of shortages.

Keep in mind, each island speaks a different language. If the data were passed around in several languages, each island would need to invest in researchers to learn all the world's languages and employ a team of translators. This would be expensive and time consuming. This is an intelligent world, however, so the islands all agreed on a single language with a standard format for communicating their trade data. Each island employs just a single translator that understands the one data format of the trade reports brought by the carrier seagulls.

The real world of technology is much like the imagined island world example. There is a vast ocean, full of islands that have different languages, customs, and architecture. The ability for these unique systems to communicate is integral to many businesses and organizations. If each of these systems needed a translator for all the many ways other systems structure their data, then communications would consume an unreasonable amount of time and resources. Instead, the systems agree on a single format for data and employ a single translator.

JSON is a data interchange format that many systems have agreed on using for communicating data. You may hear it referred to as a "data exchange format," or simply a "data format." In this book, I will refer to JSON as a data interchange format because the definition of "interchange" reminds us that the data format is intended for two or more entities exchanging it.

Many, but not all systems have agreed on JSON for communicating data. There are data interchange formats, such as Extensible Markup Language (XML), that were around before JSON was even thought about. The real world is not quite as simple as the island example. Many systems have and still use other formats, such as XML, or more tabular, delimited formats such as comma-separated values (CSV). The decision by each island in the real world for which data format to accept for communication often has to do with how the data format relates to the customs, language, and architecture of the island.

In the island world example, each of the hundreds of islands had its own language. The data in the paper report that the carrier seagulls carried was in an agreed upon format that was independent of language. This way, a single translator of the trade reports data could be employed by each island. The same is true of JSON, except the data is carried across networks in zeros and ones instead of by seagulls. The translator isn't a human, it is a parser employed by the system consuming the data so it can be read within the system it is entering.

JSON Is Programming Language Independent

JSON stands for JavaScript Object Notation. The name of this data interchange format may mislead people into thinking they will need to learn JavaScript to understand and use JSON. There would be some value in learning JavaScript before learning JSON, as it was born out of a subset of JavaScript, but if you will not be using JavaScript anytime soon it would be unnecessary. You may remain dedicated to the language or languages of your own island, for the spirit of a data interchange format is to be independent of language.

JSON is based on JavaScript object literals. A detailed explanation into the "how" of this is better suited for our discussion on syntax (Chapter 2) and data types (Chapter 3). For this chapter, the "why" is important. If a data interchange format is meant to be language independent, then it may seem contradictory to have a data format that is not only derived from a single language, but advertises it in its name: JavaScript Object Notation. Why, then?

If we return to the island example, imagine for a moment what the meeting to select the data format would have been like. When the representatives from each of the hundreds of islands arrived at this meeting, and looked to create a single data format, the first thing they would want to find is common ground.

The languages of each island may have been unique, but there were things the islanders found they had in common. Most of the languages were spoken primarily with the human voice and included a written form of the language represented by characters of some sort. Additionally, facial expressions and hand movements were also present. There were a few troublesome islands where the people communicated by other means, such as hitting sticks together or winking, but the majority of the islands found common ground with their written and spoken forms of language.

In the real world, there are hundreds of programming languages. Some are more popular and commonly used than others, but the language landscape is diverse. When college students major in computer science in preparation for a career in programming, they do not study all the programming languages. Students usually begin with one language, and the language itself is not so important as learning the universally accepted programming concepts. Once students gain an understanding of these concepts, they can more easily learn other programming languages through their ability to recognize the common features and functionalities.

If we set aside the word "JavaScript" from the name "JavaScript Object Notation," we would be left with "Object Notation." In fact, let's forget JavaScript all together. We could then say we are using an object notation data interchange format. "Object" is a common programming concept, in particular to object-oriented programming (OOP). Most computer science students studying programming will learn the concept of objects.

Without diving into an explanation of objects, let's settle our attention on the word "Notation." *Notation* implies a system of characters for representing data such as numbers or words. With or without an understanding of objects in programming, it is not a stretch to see the value of having a notation to describe something that is common across programming languages.

Returning again to the island example, the islanders themselves found a notation that represented a common tie among the majority of languages. Most of the islanders had a similar way of representing numbers with tallies, and it was agreed they could understand a series of symbols for representing real-world objects such as wheat or fabric. Even the island that communicated by winking found this format acceptable.

Despite the agreement among the vast majority of islands, there were still a few islands, such as the island that communicated by hitting sticks together, that did not find the format understandable. A good data interchange format covers the majority, but there are usually outliers. When we talk about this coverage, a term often thrown around is *portability*. Portability, or the compatibility in transferring information between platforms and systems, is the very goal of a data interchange format.

Circling back to notation, the notation of JSON may originate from JavaScript, but the notation itself is the important part. Not only is JSON language independent, it represents data in a way that speaks to common elements of many programming languages. With the way that data is represented, such as numbers and words, even the programming languages that aren't object oriented can find this format acceptable.

Key Terms and Concepts

This chapter covered the following key terms:

JSON
JavaScript Object Notation.

Notation
A system of characters for representing data such as numbers or words.

Data interchange format
Text used to exchange data between platforms or systems.

Portability
Transferring information between platforms in a way that is compatible with both systems.

We also discussed these key concepts:

- JSON is a data interchange format.
- JSON is programming language independent (JavaScript is not required to use it).
- JSON is based on the object literal notation of JavaScript (emphasis on the word "notation").
- JSON represents data in a way that is friendly to universal programming concepts.

CHAPTER 2

JSON Syntax

JSON Is Based on JavaScript Object Literals

In the English language, the word "literal" is an adjective used to imply that what is being said is exact, not a metaphor. When your friend says, "She showed up out of nowhere and I literally dropped my sandwich," he is stating that the dropping of the sandwich is not a metaphor.

In programming, the word "literal" is a noun. A *literal* is a value that is represented literally with data. It is written precisely as it is meant to be interpreted. If you aren't familiar with programming concepts, then this might seem strange. Let's take a quick look at literals.

Do you carry cash in your wallet, or a debit card? When I stop off at the sandwich shop and hand the cashier a five dollar bill for my sandwich, I physically watch my five dollars leave my wallet. When I swipe my debit card to pay for a sandwich, I know I have five dollars less in my back account, even though I didn't see it happen.

In programming, we often use variables to represent values. For example, I might use a *variable* I call x in an expression like:

```
x = 5
```

Then, later on, I might want to add five more to x:

```
x = x + 5
```

At this point, we know the value of x is 10, but we don't *see* 10. In this example, x was the variable, and 5 was a literal. In our sandwich shop example, we could say that the five dollars cash was a literal, and the debit card was a variable. When we *see* the actual value, it is a literal value.

In the "$x = 5$" example, 5 is a number literal. A number is a data type. Other types of data are strings (made up of characters), boolean (true or false), null (nothing), collections of values, and objects. Representing a number value in a way that we can see is simple, and we use a number character. Representing a boolean value is also simple and we can use true/false or 0/1. If you are familiar with the concept of objects, you will understand that representing an object is no easy or simple matter. If you aren't familiar with the concept of objects, that is OK too.

In programming, the concept of an object is similar to how you would describe a real-world object, such as your shoes. You could describe your shoes with attributes or properties such as color, style, brand, and the type of insole. Some of these attribute values could be a number, such as shoe size, and others could be a boolean (true/false) such as "has laces." Example 2-1 shows an example.

Example 2-1. Using JSON to describe the shoes I'm wearing right now

```
{
    "brand": "Crocs",
    "color": "pink",
    "size": 9,
    "hasLaces": false
}
```

Don't be concerned just yet about the syntax in the shoe example; we will arrive there later in this chapter. The main point of the shoe example is that you (even a human) can literally read the attributes of my shoe. The data type for my JSON shoe example is object. The literal value of the object exposes the properties or attributes in a way which we can see (and read). These attributes or properties of the shoe object are represented as name-value pairs.

JSON is based on JavaScript object literals. The key phrase here is "based on." In JavaScript (and most programming languages with objects), the object can include a function. So not only could I represent the properties of my shoe with the JavaScript object, but I could create a function called "walk."

However, data interchange is about data, so JSON does not include the functions of JavaScript object literals. The way that JSON is based on JavaScript object literals is purely in the syntactic representation of the object literal and its properties. This representation of properties is achieved with name-value pairs.

Name-Value Pairs

The concept of name-value pairs is widespread in computing. They are called by other names as well: key-value pairs, attribute-value pairs, and field-value pairs. In this book, we will refer to them as name-value pairs.

If you are familiar with the concept of name-value pairs, JSON will seem natural to you. If you aren't familiar with name-value pairs, that's OK too. Let's take a quick look at name-value pairs.

In a name-value pair, you first declare the name. For example, "animal". Now, pair implies two things: a name and a value. So let's give our name (in this case, "animal") a value. To simplify this concept for this chapter, let's use a string value. With name-value pairs in JSON, the value can also be a number, a boolean, null, an array, or an object. We will go more in depth with the other value data types beyond string in Chapter 3. So, for this name-value pair, which has the name "animal", we will use the string value, "cat":

```
"animal" : "cat"
```

"animal" is the name and "cat" is the value. There are many ways that we could choose to delimit, or separate, the name and the value. If I were to provide you with a directory of a company's employees with their job titles, I'd probably hand you a list that looks something like this:

- Bob Barker, Chief Executive Officer
- Janet Jackson, Chief Operations Officer
- Mr. Ed, Chief Financial Officer

For my employee directory, I used commas to separate my job titles (names) and employee names (values). I also placed the value on the left and the name on the right.

JSON uses the colon character (:) to separate the names and values. The name is always on the left and the value is always on the right. Let's take a look at a few more:

```
"animal" : "horse"
```

```
"animal" : "dog"
```

Simple, right? A name and a value, and you have a name-value pair.

Proper JSON Syntax

Now let's take a look at what proper JSON syntax entails. The name, which in our example is "animal", is always surrounded in double quotes. The name in the double quotes can be any valid string. So, you could have a name that looks like this, and it would be perfectly valid JSON:

```
"My animal": "cat"
```

You can even place an apostrophe in the name:

```
"Lindsay's animal": "cat"
```

Now that you know that this is valid JSON, I'm going to tell you why you shouldn't do this. The name-value pairs used in JSON are a friendly data structure to many systems. Having a space or special character (other than a–z, 0–9) in the name would not be taking *portability* into consideration. In Chapter 1, we defined this key term as "transferring information between platforms in a way that is compatible with both systems." We can do things in our JSON data that decrease portability; therefore, we say it is important to avoid spaces or special characters for *maximum portability*.

The name in the name-value pair of your JSON, if it is to be loaded in memory by a system as an object, will become a "property" or "attribute." A property or attribute in some systems can include an underscore character (_) or numbers, but in most cases it is considered good form to stick to the characters of the alphabet, A–Z or a–z. So, if I wanted to include multiple words in my name, I would format like so:

```
"lindsaysAnimal": "cat"
```

or

```
"myAnimal": "cat"
```

The "cat" value in the example has double quotes. Unlike the name in the name-value pair, the value does not always have double quotes. If our value is a string data type, we must have double quotes. In JSON, the remaining data types are number, boolean, array, object, and null. These will not be surrounded in double quotes. The format of these will be covered in Chapter 3.

JSON stands for JavaScript Object Notation. So, the only thing we are missing is the syntax that makes it an object. We need curly brackets surrounding our name-value pair to make it an object. So, one before…

```
{ "animal" : "cat" }
```

…and one after. When you are formatting your JSON, picture a knighting ceremony where the master of the ceremony dubs the new knight on the shoulders with a sword. You are the master of the ceremony, and you must dub your JSON as an object on each side with a curly bracket. "I dub thee, sir JSON." The ceremony would not be complete without a tap on each shoulder.

In JSON, multiple name-value pairs are separated by a comma. So, to extend the animal/cat example, let's add a color:

```
{ "animal" : "cat", "color" : "orange" }
```

Another way to look at JSON syntax would be through the eyes of the machine that is reading it. Unlike humans, machines are very rigidly rule- and instruction-oriented creatures. When you use any of the following characters outside of a string value (not surrounded in quotes), you are providing an instruction on how your data is to be read:

- { (left curly bracket) says "begin object"
- } (right curly bracket) says "end object"
- [(left square bracket) says "begin array"
-] (right square bracket) says "end array"
- : (colon) says "separating a name and a value in a name-value pair"
- , (comma) says "separating a name-value pair in an object" or "separating a value in an array"; can also be read as "here comes another one"

If you forget to say "end object" with a right curly bracket, then your object will not be recognized as an object. If you place a comma at the end of your list of name-value pairs, you are giving the instruction "here comes another one" and then not providing it. Therefore, it is important to be correct in your syntax.

A Story: The Double Quotes of JSON

One day I was peering over a student's shoulder, looking at his computer screen. He was showing me some JSON that he was about to validate (Example 2-2).

Example 2-2. The "JSON" that would not validate

```
{
    title : "This is my title.",
    body : "This is the body."
}
```

Upon validation he received a parsing error and became frustrated. He said, "Look, there's nothing wrong with it!"

I pointed out to him that he was missing quotes around "title" and "body". He said, "But I've seen JSON formatted both ways, with and without quotes around the names." "Ah," I said. "When you saw it without quotes around the names, that was not JSON. It was a JavaScript object."

This confusion is understandable. JSON is based on JavaScript object literals, so it looks much the same. A JavaScript object literal does not need quotes around the name of the name-value pair. In JSON, it is absolutely required.

Another point of confusion can be the usage of single quotes instead of double quotes. In JavaScript, an object may have single quotes for syntax instead of double quotes (see Example 2-3).

Example 2-3. This is not valid JSON

```
{
    'title': 'This is my title.',
    'body': 'This is the body.'
}
```

In JSON, only double quotes are used, and they are absolutely required around the name of the name-value pair (see Example 2-4).

Example 2-4. Valid JSON

```
{
    "title": "This is my title.",
    "body": "This is the body."
}
```

Syntax Validation

Unlike machines, as a human using a keyboard, creating an error is as simple as a missed keystroke. It's amazing, really, that we don't produce more errors than we do. Validating JSON is an important part of working with JSON.

Your integrated development environment (IDE) might have built-in validation for your JSON. If your IDE supports plug-ins and add-ons, you might find a validation tool there if it is not already integrated. If you don't use an IDE, or have no idea what I'm talking about, that's OK too.

There are many online tools for formatting and validating JSON. A quick jaunt on your search engine for "JSON validation" will give you several results. Here are a few worth mentioning:

JSON Formatter & Validator (http://jsonformatter.curiousconcept.com/)
   A formatting tool with options, and a beautiful UI that highlights errors. The processed JSON displays in a window that doubles as a tree/node style visualization tool and a window to copy/paste your formatted code from.

JSON Editor Online (https://www.jsoneditoronline.org/)
   An all-in-one validation, formatting, and visualization tool for JSON. An error indicator is displayed on the line of the error. Upon validation, helpful parsing error information is displayed. The visualization tool displays your JSON in a tree/node format.

JSONLint (http://jsonlint.com/)
   A no-bells-and-whistles validation tool for JSON. Simply copy, paste, and click "validate." It also kindly formats your JSON.

These are tools for *syntax validation*. Later, in Chapter 4, we'll discuss another type of validation called conformity validation. Syntax validation concerns the form of JSON itself, whereas conformity validation concerns a unique data structure. For Example 2-5, syntax validation would be concerned that our JSON is correct (surrounded in curly brackets, dividing our name-value pairs with commas). Conformity validation would be concerned that our data included a name, breed, and age. Additionally the conformity validation would be concerned that the value of age is a number, and the value of name is a string.

Example 2-5. Validation example

```
{
    "name": "Fluffy",
    "breed": "Siamese",
    "age": 2
}
```

JSON as a Document

You might find that in your future experiences with JSON, you are only ever creating it in code and passing it around in an unseen world that can only be inspected by developer tools. However, as a data interchange format, JSON can be its own document and live in a filesystem. The file extension for JSON is easy to remember: *.json*.

So, if I were to save my animal/cat JSON to a file and store it on my computer, it would look something like this: *C:\animals.json*.

The JSON MediaType

Oftentimes when you are passing data to someone else, you need to tell them ahead of time what type it is. You may hear this called an Internet media type, a content type, or a MIME type. This type is formatted as *type/subtype*. One type that you may have already heard of is `text/html`.

The MIME type for JSON is `application/json`.

The Internet Assigned Numbers Authority (IANA) maintains a comprehensive list of media types (*http://www.iana.org/assignments/media-types/media-types.xhtml*).

Key Terms and Concepts

This chapter covered the following key terms:

Literal
    A value that is written precisely as it is meant to be interpreted.

Variable
    A value that can be changed and is represented by an identifier, such as x.

Maximum portability (in data interchange)
    Transcending the base portability of the data format by ensuring the data itself will be compatible across systems or platforms.

Name-value pair
> A name-value pair (or key-value pair) is a property or attribute with a name, and a corresponding value.

Syntax validation
> Validation concerned with the form of JSON.

Conformity validation
> Validation concerned with the unique data structure.

We also discussed these key concepts:

- JSON is based on the syntactic representation of the properties of JavaScript object literals. This *does not* include the functions of JavaScript object literals.
- In the JSON name-value pair, the name is always surrounded by double quotes.
- In the JSON name-value pair, the value can be a string, number, boolean, null, object, or array.
- The list of name-value pairs in JSON is surrounded by curly brackets.
- In JSON, multiple name-value pairs are separated by a comma.
- JSON files use the *.json* extension.
- The JSON media type is `application/json`.

CHAPTER 3

JSON Data Types

If you've already learned a programming language or two, you likely have an under-standing of data types. If not, that's OK too. Let's take a quick look.

Quick Look at Data Types

Imagine what would happen if you hand a little boy that knows nothing about tools a hammer, and you don't tell him what it's for. Property and bodily damage would likely occur. If this child is well behaved and coordinated, we could give this child a set of instructions for using the hammer. Instead of running around damaging things, the child would only ever use it for hammering nails and removing them (it's a well-behaved child, remember). Additionally, when you say to the child, "Will you pass me the hammer, please?", he doesn't hand you the screwdriver. Knowing what something is ahead of time and how to use it is as useful in computing as it is in the real world.

In computing, we most often need to know what type of data we are dealing with because we can do different things with different types of data. I can multiply a num-ber by another number, but I can't multiply a word by another number. If I have a list of words, I can sort them alphabetically. I can't sort the number 5 alphabetically. So, in programming, when a method (or function) says, "Will you pass me the number, please?", if we know what a number is, we won't make the mistake of passing it the word "ketchup."

In computer science, there is a set of data types referred to as primitive data types. The word "primitive" evokes imagery of Stone Age cavemen sitting around a fire grunting and sharpening sticks. It's not that these data types are unrefined like the cavemen; rather, it's that they are some of the first, most basic types of data. Like modern man and cavemen, some of the more modern and progressive data types in existence have their roots in these primitive data types:

- Numbers (e.g., 5 or 5.09)
  — Integer
  — Floating-point number
  — Fixed-point number
- Characters and strings (e.g., "a" or "A" or "apple")
- Booleans (i.e., true or false)

In different programming languages, the types of data that are "set in stone" are often referred to as the primitive data types, or the built-in types, of that language. This means that the definition of the type and what can be done with it is unchangeable. The programming language isn't going to allow you to redefine what it means to add two numbers together. These primitive data types vary from language to language, and will often include additions to the preceding list, such as a byte or reference (or pointer, or handler).

Beyond the primitive data types, there are other data types that are used in most programming languages. These are often referred to as composite data types, because they are a fusion, or compound, of the primitive data types. Composite data types, like a sandcastle, have a structure to them. If we took apart the sandcastle, we could see that the structure was built with sand, sticks, and water. If we took apart the data structure of a composite data type, we would find that it was built with our primitive data types.

One example of a composite data type that is commonly used in programming languages is an enumeration data type. Earlier, I mentioned the sorting of a list alphabetically. A list of words could be represented with different data types in different programming languages (e.g., a list or an array). If we took apart this data structure, we would find that it is made up of the primitive data types of characters or strings. The enumeration data type is a data structure that you can enumerate. I can mention each thing in the structure one by one and I can also count how many there are. See Example 3-1.

Example 3-1. "Let me enumerate the fine qualities of your personality" could be represented in programming as an array literal

```
[
    "witty",
    "charming",
    "brave",
    "bold"
]
```

You don't need to understand the array literal data structure in this example to see that we can mention each of these "fine qualities" one by one, and also establish that there are four of them.

Another composite data type is the object data type. In Chapter 2, we explored the object data type, because JavaScript Object Notation is based on the object literal notation of JavaScript. Additionally, I used JSON to describe the shoes I was wearing (see Example 3-2).

Example 3-2. My shoe described in JSON

```
{
    "brand": "Crocs",
    "color": "pink",
    "size": 9,
    "hasLaces": false
}
```

This object literal allows us to see that the object data type here is made up of name-value pairs. If we were to deconstruct this data structure, we would see that it is made up of the primitive data types: string, number, and boolean. Our names ("brand", "color", "size", "hasLaces") in our name-value pairs are all string data types. The values "Crocs" and "pink" are both of the string data type. The value "9" is of the number data type. The value "false" is of the boolean data type.

The JSON Data Types

Though programming languages may vary when it comes to composite types, and even a little when it comes to additional primitive types, most share those primitive types I mentioned earlier in the chapter:

- Numbers (e.g., 5 or 5.09)
  - — Integer
  - — Floating-point number
  - — Fixed-point number
- Characters and strings (e.g., "a" or "A" or "apple")
- Booleans (i.e., true or false)

The object data type is a data structure that is common to some of the more popular programming languages, such as Java and C#, but not all. With JSON being based on object literal notation and the object data type, you'd think this would be problematic for a data interchange format. After all, the goal of a data format is communicating between two different systems and common ground should be expressed in that format. Remember that the data structure that is the composite data type object can be deconstructed into the primitive types. Even to programming languages that do not have the object data type, once the object data structure is deconstructed into those native types, it is quite friendly.

The JSON data types are:

- Object
- String
- Number
- Boolean
- Null
- Array

The JSON Object Data Type

The JSON object data type is simple. JSON, at its root, is an object. It is a list of name-value pairs surrounded in curly braces. When you create a name-value pair within your JSON that is also an object, your JSON will begin to look nested. In Example 3-3, this is illustrated with a person described with nested objects.

Example 3-3. Nested objects

```
{
    "person": {
        "name": "Lindsay Bassett",
        "heightInInches": 66,
        "head": {
            "hair": {
                "color": "light blond",
                "length": "short",
                "style": "A-line"
            },
            "eyes": "green"
        }
    }
}
```

The top-level name-value pair here is person, with the value of an object. This object has three name-value pairs: "name", "heightInInches", and "head". The "name" name-value pair has a string value of "Lindsay Bassett". The "heightInInches" name-value pair has a number value. The "head" name-value pair has an object value. The "hair" name-value pair has an object value as well, with three string data typed name-value pairs: "color", "length", and "style". The "head" object also has an "eyes" name-value pair with a value of "green".

The JSON String Data Type

We briefly explored the JSON string data type earlier in this book with the animal/cat example:

```
{ "animal" : "cat" }
```

The value "cat" has a string data type. In the real world, unless this data is for a pet shop, the string values in the data won't be quite as simple. Even a pet shop might have more to say in its data than a single word like "cat." Perhaps the shop wants to pass along the details of its latest promotion:

> Today at Bob's Best Pets you can get a free 8 oz. sample bag of Bill's Kibble with your purchase of a puppy. Just say "Bob's the best!" at checkout.

The JSON string can be comprised of any of the Unicode characters, and all the characters in that promotional text are valid. A string value must always be surrounded in *double* quotes.

In "A Story: The Double Quotes of JSON" on page 9 in Chapter 2, I mentioned that single quotes around a string value are not valid (Example 3-4).

Example 3-4. This is not valid JSON

```
{
    'title': 'This is my title.',
    'body': 'This is the body.'
}
```

This can be confusing, especially if you've seen JavaScript object literals in the past that use single quotes. In JavaScript, we are allowed to use single quotes or double quotes interchangeably. However, it is important to remember that JSON is not a JavaScript object literal; it is only *based on* JavaScript object literals. In JSON, only double quotes are allowed for surrounding a string value.

Also mentioned in the previous chapter was how JSON is read by a parser. In the eyes of a parser, when a value begins with a double quote ("), it expects a string of text that will be ended by another double quote. This poses a problem if the string of text contains double quotes in it.

For example, suppose we're running a pet shop promotion where customers need to say "Bob's the best!" at checkout to receive a free bag of kibble. If we use the code in Example 3-5, we would run into a problem, because we can't simply surround the promotional data in double quotes.

Example 3-5. This code won't work

```
{
    "promo": "Say "Bob's the best!" at checkout for free 8oz bag of kibble."
}
```

There are quotes inside of the value, and the parser is going to read that first quote character in front of "Bob" in the promotional text as the end of the string. Then, when the parser finds the remainder of the text just hanging out there and not belonging to a name-value pair, it will produce an error. To deal with this, we must escape our quote inside of any string value by preceding it with a backslash character (\), as shown in Example 3-6.

Example 3-6. Using a backslash character to escape quotes inside of strings fixes the problem

```
{
    "promo": "Say \"Bob's the best!\" at checkout for free 8oz bag of kibble."
}
```

This backslash character will tell the parser that the quote is not the end of the string. Once the parser actually loads the string into memory, any backslash character that precedes a quote character will be removed and the text will come out on the other side as intended.

Quotes are not the only thing that need escaping when it comes to the JSON string. Because the backslash character is used to escape other characters, we must also escape the backslash. For example, the JSON shown in Example 3-7, which is meant to communicate the location of my *Program Files* directory, will produce an error. To fix this problem, we must escape the backslash character by adding another backslash character, as shown in Example 3-8.

Example 3-7. The backslash used in this code will throw an error

```
{
    "location": "C:\Program Files"
}
```

Example 3-8. The backslash character must be escaped with another backslash character

```
{
    "location": "C:\\Program Files"
}
```

In addition to the double quote and backslash characters, you must escape the following characters:

- \/ (forward slash)
- \b (backspace)
- \f (form feed)
- \t (tab)
- \n (new line)
- \r (carriage return)
- \u followed by hexadecimal characters (e.g., the smiley emoticon, \u263A)

The JSON shown in Example 3-9 will produce a parser error because the tab and new line characters must be escaped. Example 3-10 shows how to fix the problem.

Example 3-9. The tab and new line characters used in this JSON will cause an error

```
{
    "story": "\t Once upon a time, in a far away land \n there lived a princess."
}
```

Example 3-10. JSON with tab and new line characters escaped

```
{
    "story": "\\t Once upon a time, in a far away land \\n there lived a princess."
}
```

The JSON Number Data Type

Numbers are a common piece of information to pass around in data. Inventory, money, latitude/longitude, and Earth's mass are all data that can be represented as numbers; see Example 3-11.

Example 3-11. Representing numbers in JSON

```
{
    "widgetInventory": 289,
    "sadSavingsAccount": 22.59,
    "seattleLatitude": 47.606209,
    "seattleLongitude": -122.332071,
    "earthsMass": 5.97219e+24
}
```

A number in JSON can be an integer, decimal, negative number, or an exponent.

My widget inventory is 289. Inventory is typically represented by an integer (or whole number). I don't typically sell a half of something, so my inventory number will never include a decimal point.

My sad savings account contains $22.59. Though some programming languages do have a data type for money, we typically represent money in JSON as a decimal number and omit the $.

If you take a look at the latitude and longitude for the City of Seattle, you will see they are both decimal numbers, and the longitude is a negative decimal number. Negative numbers are represented with the standard minus sign character preceding the number.

Additionally, I'm representing the very large number of Earth's mass in kg using E Notation. E Notation is particularly great for scientific data and is a supported number.

The JSON Boolean Data Type

In the English language, two of the simplest answers we have for questions are "yes" or "no." If you ask your friend the question, "Would you like toast with your eggs?", he will answer "yes" or "no."

In computer programming, the boolean data type is simple. It is either true or false. If you ask your computer, "Would you like toast with your eggs?", it will answer "true" or "false."

In some programming languages, the literal value for true can be 1, and 0 for false. Sometimes the literal value characters use casing—for example, True or TRUE, and false or FALSE. In JSON, the literal value for the boolean data type is always all lowercase: true or false. Any other casing will produce an error. In Example 3-12, booleans are used to communicate data about my preferences for breakfast and lunch.

Example 3-12. Preferences

```
{
    "toastWithBreakfast": false,
    "breadWithLunch": true
}
```

The JSON null Data Type

When we have nothing of something, you might think it appropriate to say there is zero of that something. Right now, I own zero watches. The thing is, zero is a number. This implies we were counting in the first place.

What if there was a standard format of describing someone's wrist in JSON, which included some attributes? See Examples 3-13 and 3-14.

Example 3-13. Next-door neighbor Bob's might look like this

```
{
    "freckleCount": 0,
    "hairy": true,
    "watchColor": "blue"
}
```

Example 3-14. Mine would look like this

```
{
    "freckleCount": 1,
    "hairy": false,
    "watchColor": null
}
```

I don't have a watch color because I'm not wearing a watch. In programming, null is a way of saying zero, zilch, and none without having to use a number. The value for watch color cannot be defined, therefore it is null.

null should not, however, be confused with undefined, which you might run across in JavaScript. undefined is not a JSON data type, but in JavaScript, undefined is what you get when you try to access an object or a variable that does not exist at all. In JavaScript, undefined has a relationship with an object or variable with both its declared name and value not existing, and null has a relationship only with a value of an object or a variable. null is a value that means "no value." In JSON, null must always be all lowercase characters.

The JSON Array Data Type

Now let's explore the array data type. If you aren't familiar with arrays, that's OK. Let's take a quick look at what an array is.

Imagine a container that holds a dozen eggs. The container has 12 available compartments for eggs. When I first bought the eggs, there were 12. This would be an array of size 12, containing 12 eggs. See Example 3-15.

Example 3-15. This is an array of strings (for the sake of simplicity, I will use the string "egg" for each of the eggs in the compartments)

```
{
    "eggCarton": [
        "egg",
        "egg",
        "egg",
        "egg",
        "egg",
        "egg",
```

```
            "egg",
            "egg",
            "egg",
            "egg",
            "egg",
            "egg"
        ]
}
```

Notice that I have a name-value pair. The name is `"eggCarton"` and the value is an array. The array is always surrounded in square brackets (`[]`). Inside the array, we have a list, and each list item is separated by a comma. This might look similar to how we format our name-value pairs, but the key difference is that it is a list of only values. These values can be any of the valid JSON data types (string, number, object, boolean, array, and null).

Now suppose I take out two eggs to make myself eggs over easy with toast for breakfast. My egg carton still has 12 compartments, but two eggs are missing. See Example 3-16.

Example 3-16. I've removed two eggs from the carton to make breakfast

```
{
    "eggCarton": [
        "egg",
        null,
        "egg",
        "egg",
        "egg",
        "egg",
        "egg",
        "egg",
        "egg",
        "egg",
        null,
        "egg"
    ]
}
```

As you can see, I removed the eggs from two specific compartments. Those compartments became empty because the eggs no longer exist. We represent this with `null`.

An array has an index for each of the "compartments." We begin with 0, so the first compartment has an index of 0, the second has an index of 1, and so on. The last compartment will have an index of 11. So, I removed the eggs at the indices of 1 and 10. This is a valid array.

If I put the number 5 in the empty compartment at index 10, in most programming languages this would be an invalid array. See Example 3-17.

Example 3-17. This would not be valid in most programming languages

```
{
    "eggCarton": [
        "egg",
        null,
        "egg",
        "egg",
        "egg",
        "egg",
        "egg",
        "egg",
        "egg",
        "egg",
        5,
        "egg"
    ]
}
```

I said "most programming languages," but in JSON, the mixing and matching of data types is valid. I will tell you why, and then I will tell you why you shouldn't do this in your JSON.

In JavaScript, you define a variable. For instance, in Example 3-18, we have a variable named something and we assign it the number 5 for its value.

Example 3-18. Defining a variable in JavaScript

```
var something = 5;
```

On the very next line, we could change that variable to have a string value (Example 3-19).

Example 3-19. Changing that variable to have a string value

```
something = "bob";
```

And we could even change it to have a value of an object (Example 3-20).

Example 3-20. Changing that variable to have a value of an object

```
something = { person: "bob" };
```

The value for my var something (variable) can be a number, string, array, null, or object. In most programming languages, variables aren't allowed to be so shifty. Normally you would declare something, as either an int, a string, or an object. So, when you declared your variable called something, you would say int something = 5. You would say string something = "bob" or you would say Person something = new

Person("bob"). So in most programming languages, when you declare an array, you are declaring ahead of time what data type has to be in each of your containers, and you can't just change it around after the fact.

JSON is a data interchange format. If you hand your JSON array over to someone that is not going to be using your JSON with JavaScript, your array will cause an error when it is being parsed.

For example, suppose you attend a convention where merchants are selling collections of rocks. You have a collection of rocks to sell. A guy shows up and wants to buy your collection of 50 rocks, and he takes them, but when he gets home he finds the rock collection does not contain 50 rocks, but it contains 20 rocks, 20 sticks, and 10 pieces of gum (one of which has already been chewed).

Let's take a closer look at some examples of arrays of each data type. In JSON, the array can be any of the supported data types. So, we can have an array of strings, an array of numbers, an array of booleans, an array of objects, or an array of arrays. An array of arrays is called a multidimensional array. Let's take a look at some examples.

Suppose we have a roster with the names of students who signed up for a course. This can be represented using an array of strings (Example 3-21).

Example 3-21. Using an array of strings to represent a roster of students

```
{
    "students": [
        "Jane Thomas",
        "Bob Roberts",
        "Robert Bobert",
        "Thomas Janerson"
    ]
}
```

After the students have taken a test, we can use an array of numbers to represent their scores (Example 3-22).

Example 3-22. Using an array of numbers to represent test scores

```
{
    "scores": [
        93.5,
        66.7,
        87.6,
        92
    ]
}
```

If we need to create an answer key for a true/false test, we could use an array of booleans (Example 3-23).

Example 3-23. Using an array of booleans to represent the answers of a true/false test

```
{
    "answers": [
        true,
        false,
        false,
        true,
        false,
        true,
        true
    ]
}
```

An array of objects could be used to represent the entire test, including questions and answers (Example 3-24).

Example 3-24. Using an array of objects to represent the questions and answers of a test

```
{
    "test": [
        {
            "question": "The sky is blue.",
            "answer": true
        },
        {
            "question": "The earth is flat.",
            "answer": false
        },
        {
            "question": "A cat is a dog.",
            "answer": false
        }
    ]
}
```

To represent the scores from three different tests, an array of arrays, or a multidimensional array, could be used (Example 3-25).

Example 3-25. Using an array of arrays to represent the scores from three different tests

```
{
    "tests": [
        [
            true,
            false,
            false,
            false
        ],
        [
            true,
            true,
            true,
            true,
            false
        ],
        [
            true,
            false,
            true
        ]
    ]
}
```

Key Terms and Concepts

This chapter covered the following key terms:

JSON string data type
> A string value, like `"my string"`, surrounded in double quotes.

JSON boolean data type
> A true or false value.

JSON number data type
> A number value, like 42, that can be a positive or negative integer, decimal, or exponent.

JSON null data type
> A null value represents an empty value.

JSON array data type
> An array is a collection or list of values, and the values can have a data type of string, number, boolean, object, or array; the values in an array are surrounded by square brackets ([]) and delimited by a comma.

JSON object data type
> The object data type is a set of name-value pairs delimited by a comma and surrounded by curly brackets ({}).

We also discussed these key concepts:

- The boolean data type value of `true` or `false` in JSON is always all lowercase characters (i.e., `true`, not `True` or `TRUE`).
- The `null` data type value in JSON is always all lowercase characters (i.e., `null`, not `NULL` or `Null`).
- One key difference between an object and an array is that an object is a list or collection of name-value pairs and an array is a list or collection of values.
- Another key difference between an array and an object is that an array's values *should* all have the same data type.

CHAPTER 4

JSON Schema

In Chapter 3, we covered the JSON data types. The importance and usefulness of data types was discussed. Knowing ahead of time what something is and what it is for (remember the kid with the hammer) makes a world of difference.

In most scenarios with data interchange formats, the data is being created to send across the Internet or a network to another party. That party usually has a desired format for the document that they are expecting, including structure and data types. They will usually provide documentation that explains the format and provides examples.

Even when the most detailed, beautiful documentation is provided, it is not difficult to create errors in your data. To be clear, these aren't syntax errors we are talking about here. These are errors of misunderstanding, like "I sent an apple, and you were expecting an orange." In this book, I will refer to this type of validation as *conformity validation* so   that it may be distinguished from syntax validation.

In this scenario, the process usually plays out in the following steps:

1. You are finished creating your data and you feel confident.
2. You send your data across the Internet to the other party. Your Internet connection is slow today, and the data file you are sending is huge, so it takes several minutes.
3. You get an error response because your data was not formatted how they were expecting it. Confidence deflated. If you're lucky, the error response will tell you something meaningful, like what you did wrong.
4. You pore over their documentation, find what you think you did wrong, fix it, and start back at step 1.

This scenario has existed with data interchange since before JSON existed. Fortunately, the people of the technology industry are problem solvers, and the concept of the schema was born.

Contracts with Validation Magic

In the real world, we often use contracts between two parties where the outcome is important. When I sign a contract that says I will complete a project for someone, the details are outlined in that contract. I agree that I will deliver the spaceship by August 31st, and the final product will have a fully functional spaceship with life support, lasers, and three engines.

Imagine now that we live in a world of wizards and magic. When the company I'm doing the project for handed me the contract, they added a bit of magic. At any time, I can tap my wand on the contract and it will tell me whether I've met my end of the bargain. I'd never have to walk into the meeting to proclaim "I'm done!" and be met with the embarrassing response of "What about the third engine you promised to put on the spaceship. Where is it?" At any time I can verify that I am *really* done with the project and walk into the meeting with confidence.

A data interchange schema is much like that imagined world of wizards and magic. Before we send our data, we can at any time validate it for conformity with the schema and find out whether our data is acceptable. When we are interchanging data with a schema, the process is much different than our scenario without the schema:

1. You validate the conformity of your data with your schema and fix any errors found. You are usually given useful information about the errors.
2. You are finished creating your data and you feel confident.
3. You send your data across the Internet and you get a success response. Mission complete.

Additionally, the JSON schema can be used on the other end of the transaction by the party that is accepting the data. A JSON schema can be a first line of defense in accepting data, to verify that the data conforms. It can answer all of these questions before the data is processed:

Are the data types of the values correct?
    We can specify that a value has to be a number, string, etc.

Does this include the required data?
    We can specify what data is required, and what is not.

Are the values in the format that I require?
    We can specify ranges, minimum and maximum.

Introduction to JSON Schema

While JSON is fairly mature, JSON Schema is still under development. As of April 2015, JSON Schema is in draft 4. This doesn't mean that you shouldn't use JSON Schema—it just means it's still evolving to better serve the world.

A JSON Schema is written with JSON, so reading or writing one is only a few steps away. In our very first name-value pair of our JSON, we must declare it as a schema document (Example 4-1).

Example 4-1. The name for this declaration will always be "$schema," and the value will always be the link for the draft version

```
{
    "$schema": "http://json-schema.org/draft-04/schema#"
}
```

The second name-value pair in our JSON Schema Document will be the title (see Example 4-2).

Example 4-2. Format for a document that represents a cat

```
{
    "$schema": "http://json-schema.org/draft-04/schema#",
    "title": "Cat"
}
```

In the third name-value pair of our JSON Schema Document, we will define the properties that we want to be included in the JSON. The "properties" value is essentially a skeleton of the name-value pairs of the JSON we want. Instead of a literal value, we have an object that defines the data type, and optionally the description (Example 4-3).

Example 4-3. Defining the properties for a cat

```
{
  "$schema": "http://json-schema.org/draft-04/schema#",
  "title": "Cat",
  "properties": {
    "name": {
      "type": "string"
    },
    "age": {
      "type": "number",
      "description": "Your cat's age in years."
    },
    "declawed": {
      "type": "boolean"
```

```
    }
  }
}
```

We can then validate that our JSON conforms to the JSON Schema (Example 4-4).

Example 4-4. This JSON conforms to our JSON Schema for "Cat"

```
{
  "name": "Fluffy",
  "age": 2,
  "declawed": false
}
```

Earlier I stated that a JSON Schema can answer the following questions:

Are the data types of the values correct?
> We can specify that a value has to be a number, string, etc.

Does this include the required data?
> We can specify what data is required, and what is not.

Are the values in the format that I require?
> We can specify ranges, minimum and maximum.

With the very simple cat example, the first question was answered. We were able to validate that the JSON for the cat "Fluffy" has the correct data types for the values of name, age, and declawed. Let's answer the second question: does this include the required data?

When we ask for data, there are often properties (or fields) that we must have values for, and others that are optional. For example, when I create a new account on a shopping website, I need to complete a shipping address form. That address form requires my name, street, city, state, and zip code. Optionally, I can include a company name, apartment number, and a second line for a street address. If I leave out one of the required fields, I cannot move forward with the account creation.

To achieve this required logic in the JSON schema, we add a fourth name-value pair after `"$schema"`, `"title"`, and `"properties"`. This name-value pair has the name `"required"` and a value of the array data type. The array includes the fields we require.

In Example 4-5, we first add another field for `"description"`. Next, we add a fourth name-value pair, `"required"`, with an array of required values for its value. `"name"`, `"age"`, and `"declawed"` are required, so we add them to this list. We leave out `"description"` because it's not required.

Example 4-5. Defining the required fields

```
{
  "$schema": "http://json-schema.org/draft-04/schema#",
  "title": "Cat",
  "properties": {
    "name": {
      "type": "string"
    },
    "age": {
      "type": "number",
      "description": "Your cat's age in years."
    },
    "declawed": {
      "type": "boolean"
    },
    "description": {
      "type": "string"
    }
  },
  "required": [
    "name",
    "age",
    "declawed"
  ]
}
```

With the addition of `"required"` to our JSON schema, the JSON in Example 4-6 is valid. This JSON conforms to our JSON schema for `"Cat"` with the required fields of `"name"`, `"age"`, and `"declawed"`. We are including the optional name-value pair, `"description"`.

Example 4-6. Valid JSON

```
{
  "name": "Fluffy",
  "age": 2,
  "declawed": false,
  "description" : "Fluffy loves to sleep all day."
}
```

We may also leave out the `"description"` field, as it's not included in the list of required fields. The JSON in Example 4-7 conforms to our JSON Schema for `"Cat"` with the required fields of `"name"`, `"age"`, and `"declawed"`.

Example 4-7. Valid JSON without the "description" field

```
{
  "name": "Fluffy",
  "age": 2,
  "declawed": false
}
```

It is important to note that if you do not include the `"required"` name-value pair in your JSON schema with the array of required names, then nothing is required. A JSON object with no name-value pairs inside it would be considered valid. Without the array of `"required"`, the JSON in Example 4-8 is considered valid for the `"Cat"` JSON Schema.

Example 4-8. Valid JSON

```
{}
```

The third and final question we can answer with our JSON schema is: are the values in the format I require? We answered the question about the data types of our values, but we often need a specific format for the type. For example, I require a username, but the username should not exceed 20 characters. Additionally, I might ask you to think of a number between 10 and 100. We can express these specific requirements in our JSON schema.

In the cat JSON, we have requirements such as name being a string and age being a number. However, we do not want someone giving us data with a really long cat name, a really short cat name, or a negative number for the cat's age. In our JSON schema, we can define a minimum length and a maximum length for a string, and a minimum for a number.

In Example 4-9, validation has been added to ensure that the cat's name is a minimum of 3 characters and a maximum of 20 characters. Additionally, we ensure that the age of the cat submitted is not a negative number.

Example 4-9. Validating the cat JSON

```
{
  "$schema": "http://json-schema.org/draft-04/schema#",
  "title": "Cat",
  "properties": {
    "name": {
      "type": "string",
      "minLength": 3,
      "maxLength" : 20
    },
    "age": {
      "type": "number",
      "description": "Your cat's age in years.",
      "minimum" : 0
    },
    "declawed": {
      "type": "boolean"
    },
    "description": {
      "type": "string"
    }
  },
  "required": [
    "name",
    "age",
    "declawed"
  ]
}
```

The JSON in Example 4-10 is not valid with the "Cat" JSON Schema because the name value exceeds the "maxLength", and the age value precedes the "minimum".

Example 4-10. Invalid JSON

```
{
  "name": "Fluffy the greatest cat in the whole wide world",
  "age": -2,
  "declawed": false,
  "description" : "Fluffy loves to sleep all day."
}
```

The JSON in Example 4-11 is valid with the cat JSON Schema and conforms to the requirements for the values.

Example 4-11. This JSON is valid

```
{
  "name": "Fluffy",
  "age": 2,
  "declawed": false,
  "description" : "Fluffy loves to sleep all day."
}
```

If we return to the comparison of a schema to a contract, you can see that the details of our contract can be very specific. The examples provided in this chapter are introductory and just the tip of the iceberg. JSON Schema even supports regular expressions (character patterns, such as an email address format) and enum (a list of possible values). If you wish to become a master of JSON Schema, visit the following pages, where you can find links to the specifications:

- The home of JSON Schema (*http://json-schema.org/*)
- JSON Schema validation specification (*http://json-schema.org/latest/json-schema-validation.html*)

There is a long and growing list of JSON Schema libraries and projects for specific programming languages and frameworks. A quick Google search of "JSON Schema Validation [insert programming language name here]" should get you what you need if you'd like to integrate JSON Schema validation into a project. Additionally, there are a few online validators, which are programming language agnostic and great for experimenting with JSON Schema:

- JSON Schema Lint (*http://jsonschemalint.com/draft4/*)
- JSON Schema Validator (*http://www.jsonschemavalidator.net/*)

If I go to the JSON Schema Lint website, I will be presented with two text areas: one for the JSON schema, and another for the JSON document to be validated. If I paste in the schema from Example 4-9 and the JSON from Example 4-10, I will see the following errors:

- Field: data.name, Error: has longer length than allowed , Value: "Fluffy the greatest cat in the whole wide world"
- Field: data.age, Error: is less than minimum, Value: -2

If I go to the JSON Schema Validator website, I am also presented with the same two text areas. Once again, if I paste in the schema from Example 4-9 and the JSON from Example 4-10, I will see errors. Additionally, the line numbers of the JSON will display a red x, showing us where the errors are at in the JSON.

- Message: String 'Fluffy the greatest cat in the whole wide world' exceeds maximum length of 20, Schema Path: #/properties/name/maxLength
- Message: Integer -2 is less than minimum value of 0, Schema Path: #/properties/age/minimum

The JSON Schema Validator not only points us to the line numbers where the error takes place, but also gives us the paths to the schema requirements that are causing the validation to fail. The two validators may have described the errors a bit differently, but both found the same errors.

Key Terms and Concepts

This chapter covered the following key term:

JSON Schema
    A virtual contract for data interchange.

We also discussed these key concepts:

- A JSON validator provides syntax validation, while JSON Schema provides conformity validation.
- JSON Schema can serve as a first line of defense in accepting data or as a time (and sanity) saving tool for the party providing the data that ensures their data will conform to what is accepted.
- A JSON Schema can answer the following three questions for conformity validation:

Are the data types of the values correct?
    We can specify that a value has to be a number, string, etc.

Does this include the required data?
    We can specify what data is required, and what is not.

Are the values in the format that I require?
    We can specify ranges, minimum and maximum.

CHAPTER 5

JSON Security Concerns

JSON alone is not much of a threat. After all, it's only a data interchange format. By itself, it is just a document, or a stream, of data. The real security concerns with JSON arise in the way that it is used. In this chapter, we will take a look at two of the most common security concerns for JSON on the Web: cross-site request forgery and cross-site scripting.

Before we move forward in discussing security concerns, and enter into the remaining chapters of this book, we need an understanding of client-side and server-side relationships. Let's take a quick look at these relationships, for those that do not yet understand this concept.

A Quick Look at Client- and Server-Side Relationships

Upon arriving at Pierre's Fine Dining for dinner, I sit down at a lovely table where the napkins are folded into swans. A tall man in slacks and a nice shirt approaches the table and says, "My name is Thomas, and I am here to serve you this evening." After he recognizes me, he lowers his voice and says, "By the way, you are one of my favorite clients." He wags his eyebrows and says, "Here is our special menu."

After perusing the special menu, I tell Thomas what I would like for dinner, and after some time he brings it to the table. I eat a lovely dinner, and then later pay $200 for the artistically arranged plates of tiny food. It was another fine evening at Pierre's Fine Dining, where Thomas was the server, and I was the client.

Your Internet browser has a relationship with websites, just like I have the relationship with Pierre's Fine Dining. This relationship is a bustling world of *requests* and *responses*. I request a plate of food, and the kitchen responds by creating the specific food I requested and sends it out to be delivered to me.

When you go to your favorite website to look at cute kitten pictures, the Internet browser on your computer is the client and the computer that hosts the cute kitten pictures is the server. Your Internet browser makes a request that travels around the Internet until the computer behind the cute kitten picture website receives it. The cute kitten website then serves up the page in a response that gets sent back across the Internet. Your browser then renders the page for you on the screen.

In this relationship, we draw a line in the sand and say that everything sent in response by the cute kitten pictures website that will be dealt with by the browser is called client-side code. In the restaurant example, the response would be the plate of food and the table where I sit would be the Internet browser. The table receives the plate of food and now I can see it and consume it.

We then say that everything that happened before that response page was sent, essentially the creation of it, is the server-side code. In the restaurant example, the server-side code would be everything that happens in the kitchen. I never go into the kitchen, and I don't see what they are doing in there to make my plate of food. The subtle difference between the restaurant example and the real world is that the server is not the guy running back and forth between the kitchen and the table. The kitchen is the server, and that guy is the Internet.

The public doesn't see what the cute kitten pictures website is doing in its metaphorical kitchen. The site could be using PHP, or ASP.NET, or any number of programming languages. Whatever it's using in its kitchen doesn't matter to my browser, so long as the site hands over a response with client-side code.

The response that I get from the site is a combination of HTML, CSS, and JavaScript. Just like I can inspect everything at the table in the restaurant, I can hit F12 in my browser, and using developer tools I can see all the HTML, CSS, and JavaScript for the page. I can even see the JavaScript code for that annoying flashing pop up with the dancing kittens.

Client side is everything happening in a user's Internet browser, and server side is everything that is happening on the server where the website is hosted. When client-side code is referred to, it usually means JavaScript, HTML, or CSS. When server-side code is referred to, it usually means server-side languages such as ASP.NET, Ruby on Rails, or Java.

Now let's take a look at the important subject of security concerns.

Cross-Site Request Forgery (CSRF)

Cross-site request forgery, or CSRF (pronounced sea-surf), is an exploit that takes advantage of a site's trust in a user's Internet browser. CSRF vulnerabilities have been around a long time, way before JSON came into existence.

An example of a CSRF exploit with JSON would be something like this.

You sign into a banking website. This website has a JSON URL that includes some sensitive information about you (Example 5-1).

Example 5-1. Your sensitive information in JSON format

```
[
    {
        "user": "bobbarker"
    },
    {
        "phone": "555-555-5555"
    }
]
```

You might think, "Hey, this JSON is missing its curly brackets!" This is valid JSON. Dangerous valid JSON because it is also a valid JavaScript script. This is called a *top-level JSON array.*

The example banking website uses authentication with session cookies to make sure that this information is only given to you—the logged in and registered user.

The bad guy in this example finds the URL to the sensitive JSON data on the banking website and puts it in a <script> tag on *his* own website. If you aren't sure what a <script> tag is, you can find them behind the scenes on most modern web pages. This is called the code-behind, and it is an HTML document. If you go to your favorite website, right-click, and select view source, you should find one or more tags that look like the one shown in Example 5-2.

Example 5-2. Example of a <script> tag (the "src" attribute in this tag specifies where the script is located)

```
<script src="https://code.jquery.com/jquery-2.1.4.min.js"></script>
```

Internet browsers have rules about sharing between websites with different domains (*http://domainone.com* and *http://domaintwo.com* are different domains). The bad guy uses the <script> tag because it is exempt from those rules about sharing (Example 5-3). It is often necessary and normal to use a script hosted by another website, so the <script> tag gets an exception. The JSON is using a top-level array that makes it valid JavaScript, so he gets away with it.

Example 5-3. Example of what the <script> tag on the bad guy's site might look like

```
<script src="https://www.yourspecialbank.com/user.json"></script>
```

One key thing for this to work is your relationship with the bank's website. Without your relationship, the link in the <script> tag won't return sensitive data. That link doesn't just host your sensitive data. It is a dynamic link, which returns the sensitive data for the member that is logged in. When you log in with the bank, you have initiated a relationship where the bank trusts that you are who you say you are.

This exploit depends on that trust. In order for the bad guy to exploit the trust, he needs you to come to his website that has the stolen <script> tag while you are logged in to your bank. To achieve this, the bad guy might send out a million emails to people that say, "There is an important message for you on your banking website." These emails will often be formatted exactly like emails that people are familiar with from their bank (or the website they are attempting to exploit). If they don't check the email headers to see who it's from, or hover over the link to question if it's going to their trusted website's real domain, then they will likely click it.

For example's sake, let's pretend you were ill and not thinking clearly, so you clicked on the link. Additionally, you didn't log out of your banking site last time you were there, so your session still exists. You are currently in a state of the trust relationship with the bank. Once the page to the bad guy's site loads, you may realize that you've landed somewhere strange and leave. By then it's too late. The bad guy's site was able to retrieve the sensitive JSON data and send it back to its own servers and keep. Ouch.

What could the bank and its web developers have done differently to prevent a CSRF exploit?

To start, the bank could have turned the array into a value in a JSON object. This would make it invalid JavaScript. See Example 5-4.

Example 5-4. By wrapping the array in an object, it is no longer valid JavaScript that can be loaded in a <script> tag

```
{
    "info": [
        {
            "user": "bobbarker"
        },
        {
            "phone": "555-555-5555"
        }
    ]
}
```

Also, if the bank had only allowed POST requests instead of GET requests to retrieve the sensitive JSON, then the bad guy couldn't have used the link in his URL. GET and POST are two HTTP methods that are used to communicate with the server. GET is a request for data, and can return a response. POST is a submission of data, and can also return a response. If a server allows a `GET` request for a link, it can be linked to directly in a browser or a `<script>` tag. `POST`, however, cannot be linked to directly. Without that handy `<script>` tag, the bad guy would have his hands tied with resource sharing policies, preventing him from doing anything else client side that could spoof the bank into trusting him.

This does not mean that HTTP data interchange with JSON should be entirely limited to the `POST` method. A good rule of thumb for deciding whether or not to allow `GET` requests for a page or resource is to ask: will this page ever need to be accessed directly by URL, or used in a `<script>` tag? If the answer is "no," then the `GET` method should be disallowed to prevent just anyone from accessing it via a URL or `<script>` tag.

Sensitive data is also key to this exploit. If the JSON only contained a list of species of birds, the bad guy probably wouldn't set up a site to attempt to steal the data. However, in being prepared for security threats, habits are important. If you don't get into the habit of using top-level arrays in your JSON, and you don't get into the habit of conveniently using `GET` instead of `POST`, then you aren't susceptible to being that person that wrote the code that caused a huge exploit and a bunch of angry customers.

Injection Attacks

Injection attacks take many shapes and forms. Ultimately, they rely on finding exploitable holes in security. The CSRF attack that was just covered was an attack that relied on trust. An *injection attack* is an attack that relies on the ability to inject malicious code into an otherwise innocent website.

Cross-Site Scripting (XSS)

Cross-site scripting (XSS) attacks are a type of injection attack. A hole in security that often takes place with JSON is at the point where the JavaScript fetches a string of JSON and turns it into a JavaScript object.

Remember that JSON by itself is just text. In programming, if we want to do anything useful with that textual representation of an object, it needs to be loaded into memory as an object. It can then be manipulated, inspected, and used in programming logic.

In JavaScript, one way to do this is by using a function called `eval()`, which takes a string, compiles it, and then executes it.

In Example 5-5, the JavaScript code uses the `eval()` function to load the animal/cat object into memory. The properties of the object can then be accessed in the code. The alert on the third line will pop up a browser alert that says "cat."

Example 5-5. Accessing object properties

```
var jsonString = '{"animal":"cat"}';
var myObject = eval("(" + jsonString + ")");
alert(myObject.animal);
```

Example 5-5 is relatively harmless because the JSON is directly in the code. Typically, the JSON would be coming from another server. This server is often a third-party server, which you have no control over. For example, if I were asking Facebook's server for some JSON, I have no control over what JSON it gives me. If the server were exploited, or the JSON intercepted somehow, I could be served malicious code.

The issue with the eval() function is it takes a string, and compiles and executes it without discrimination. If my JSON is coming from a third-party server and is replaced with a malicious script, then my perfectly innocent website will be compiling and executing this malicious code in the Internet browsers of those who visit my site.

In the JavaScript code in Example 5-6, I've replaced the JSON string with some Java-Script. When this code runs, the eval() function will execute and display an alert that says "this is bad."

Example 5-6. An alert from the eval() function

```
var jsonString = "alert('this is bad')";
var myObject = eval("(" + jsonString + ")");
alert(myObject.animal);
```

As JSON has grown up over the years this vulnerability has been recognized. The JSON.parse() function deals with this vulnerability by being discriminate. This function will only parse JSON, and will not execute scripts. Example 5-7 replaces eval() with JSON.parse().

Example 5-7. Replacing eval() with JSON.parse()

```
var jsonString = '{"animal":"cat"}';
var myObject = JSON.parse(jsonString);
alert(myObject.animal);
```

In web development, another concern that often weighs just as heavily as security concerns is cross-browser support. As the Web evolves, those who host websites must decide which browsers and which versions they should support. Essentially, they have to decide who to leave behind. There will always be people that don't update their Internet browsers, or who use a less popular Internet browser that isn't keeping up with the evolving standards.

The much safer JSON.parse() function is currently supported in all major Internet browsers and their most recent versions. However, some earlier Internet browser versions that a small percentage of users are still on do not support this function. If JSON.parse() is used, that small percentage of users will not be able to use the functionality of the website that relies on JSON. Oftentimes, this is dealt with by finding ways to gracefully fail. For example, instead of a web page full of rampant errors, consider one that catches those errors and displays a message such as "Please update your browser to the latest version."

Holes in Security: Architectural Decisions

At the beginning of the chapter, I said, "JSON by itself is not a threat." This still holds true, but there are some scenarios in which a threat can be included directly within the JSON data, while still remaining valid JSON.

Let's take a look at some perfectly innocent JSON (Example 5-8).

Example 5-8. Perfectly innocent JSON

```
{
    "message": "hello, world!"
}
```

Now let's pretend that I host a website that stores messages in a database and then displays them on a web page for a user to read. I've never heard of this exploit, so I have a page where one user can send another user a message that contains anything. On my messages page, I request the JSON string from the server, and client side I use the eval() JavaScript function to convert the JSON string response to a JavaScript object. I use that JavaScript object in my client-side code to display the message value directly in the HTML.

Let's take a look at some less innocent JSON in Example 5-9.

Example 5-9. Not-so-innocent JSON

```
{
    "message": "<div onmouseover=\"alert('gotcha!')\">hover here.</div>"
}
```

The not-so-innocent JSON in the example includes JavaScript. While this JavaScript is within the bounds of the JSON name-value pair, it is simply a string of text. This is perfectly valid JSON and there are many places where this JSON could be used that is not a threat.

However, the JavaScript in the example, when outputted within the HTML on the messaging website, is a threat. The "not-so-innocent JSON" shown here will cause an alert to pop up with the message "gotcha!" every time the user hovers their mouse cursor over the message on the screen. The problem is that far worse could be done than popping up an alert. A bad guy could include a script to access all of your private messages on the page and send them to his own server to read.

What could I have done to prevent this? For one, I could have taken measures to disallow HTML in my messages. This could involve both client-side and server-side validation. Additionally, I could ensure that any HTML characters included in the message were escaped, so the HTML characters such as <div> would display as <div> on the page (<div> would not function as valid HTML). All of these measures would be specific to the client-side and server-side code that I am using in my architecture.

Most injection attacks involve architecture that has not been built with one important question in mind: how can a bad guy exploit this? The decision to allow HTML in the JSON and display the values directly on the page was a seemingly innocent architectural decision. In avoiding injection attacks, the key is to think through possible exploits, and take the extra (and sometimes arduous) steps to prevent them.

Key Terms and Concepts

This chapter covered the following key terms:

Server side (in web development)
> The operations that take place behind the scenes on the server where a page or resource is being requested. The server provides the response that the Internet browser processes and/or loads.

Client side (in web development)
> The operations that take place in the Internet browser from the point that a requested page is loaded. This is typically HTML, CSS, and JavaScript.

Cross-site request forgery (CSRF)
> An exploit that takes advantage of a site's trust in a user's browser.

Top-level JSON array
> A JSON array that exists outside of a name-value pair and at the top level of the document.

Injection attack
> An attack that relies on injecting data into a web application to facilitate the execution or interpretation of malicious data.

JSON cross-site scripting (XSS) attack
> A type of injection attack that takes advantage of an innocent website by intercepting or replacing JSON being served to the site by a third party with a malicious script.

We also discussed these key concepts:

- JSON by itself is not a threat. It is just text.
- Three things to remember that will address security concerns with JSON:
  - Do not use top-level arrays. Top-level arrays are valid JavaScript that can be linked to in a `<script>` tag and used.
  - Use HTTP `POST` instead of `GET` for JSON that is not intended for the public. The HTTP `GET` request can be linked to in a URL and placed in a `<script>` tag.
  - Use `JSON.parse()` instead of `eval()`. The `eval()` function will compile and execute the string that is passed in, which opens your code up for attacks. `JSON.parse()` only parses JSON.
- Holes in security are often introduced through architectural decisions that do not ask the basic question of "How can a bad guy exploit this?"

CHAPTER 6

The JavaScript XMLHttpRequest and Web APIs

The JavaScript XMlHttpRequest and web APIs might be difficult to say three times fast, but it's really not as complicated as it sounds. It is a simple client and server relationship. The JavaScript XMLHttpRequest is the client making the requests, and the web API is the server sending the responses.

In the client–server restaurant example discussed in the previous chapter, I referred to the server as the kitchen and the client as the customer. This chapter will focus on a type of kitchen and how this kitchen operates.

It goes without saying that not every restaurant operates the same. In some restaurants, you can drive up to a window to order your food. Some restaurants are open to the public and other restaurants may only serve as a cafeteria inside of a large company campus.

A client–server relationship that most of us participate in is surfing the Internet. Oftentimes we think of ourselves as traveling, or exploring around the Internet. In reality, we are usually sitting and staring into a screen. The Internet browser isn't going anywhere either. It just sits in place, as if at a table in a restaurant, making requests and receiving responses. Once the server gives us our response, it is done with us and moves on to some other entity making a request.

The request being made by the Internet browser is for a resource. When we are "surfing the Internet," we either click a link with a URL or we directly type in a URL in our browser. URL stands for Universal *Resource* Locator. The URLs we use in our Internet browsing are for locating HTML resources, which allows us to see our websites, including the one with pictures of cute kittens. In this scenario, the resource we are requesting has a content type of text/html.

Another client–server relationship that doesn't directly involve humans is a web API. A web API serves content over HTTP just like a website does, but it is not meant for human eyes. You can think of it as a restaurant that caters to code because the majority of requests to these servers are made by code.

Programming code doesn't usually order up pictures of cute kittens to look at like we do. Its appetite usually consists of requesting data. This chapter is about a type of client that orders up JSON (a resource with a content type of `application/json`), and the type of restaurant that caters to these customers: web APIs.

Let's begin by taking a look at web APIs, and the role JSON has within a web API.

Web APIs

Unlike humans, code doesn't have a pair of eyes that want to read an article or view a picture. Code needs to view that "something" in a format that it can read (parse). This is where a data interchange format (like JSON, shown in Example 6-1) steps into the picture.

Example 6-1. JSON weather data from the OpenWeatherMap web API

```
{
    "dt": 1433383200,
    "temp": {
        "day": 293.5,
        "min": 293.5,
        "max": 293.5,
        "night": 293.5,
        "eve": 293.5,
        "morn": 293.5
    },
    "pressure": 1015.06,
    "humidity": 98,
    "weather": [
        {
            "id": 802,
            "main": "Clouds",
            "description": "scattered clouds",
            "icon": "03n"
        }
    ],
    "speed": 2.86,
    "deg": 134,
    "clouds": 44
}
```

The JSON weather data example can be "read" by any code capable of parsing JSON. This JSON resource can be requested with a URL (the code example is a subset of the full JSON document):

http://api.openweathermap.org/data/2.5/forecast/daily?
lat=35&lon=139&cnt=10&mode=json

Though many public web APIs like OpenWeatherMap are for "reading," many APIs such as the PayPal API are more interactive. A *web API* is a set of instructions and standards for interacting with a service over HTTP. That interaction can include create, read, update, and delete (CRUD) operations and the web API will have a reference outlining these instructions and standards.

For example, according to the PayPal API reference, I can create a new invoice with the PayPal API by posting JSON to the URL:

https://api.sandbox.paypal.com/v1/invoicing/invoices

In Example 6-2, we have JSON representing an invoice to be sent as a request to the PayPal API.

Example 6-2. An invoice for the PayPal API

```json
{
    "merchant_info": {
        "email": "bob@bob.com",
        "first_name": "Bob",
        "last_name": "Bobberson",
        "business_name": "Bob Equipment, LLC",
        "phone": {
            "country_code": "001",
            "national_number": "5555555555"
        },
        "address": {
            "line1": "123 Fake St.",
            "city": "Somewhere",
            "state": "OR",
            "postal_code": "97520",
            "country_code": "US"
        }
    },
    "billing_info": [
        {
            "email": "someguy@someguy.com"
        }
    ],
    "items": [
        {
            "name": "Widgets",
            "quantity": 20,
            "unit_price": {
```

```
                    "currency": "USD",
                    "value": 89
                }
            }
        ],
        "note": "Special Widgets Order!",
        "payment_term": {
            "term_type": "NET_45"
        },
        "shipping_info": {
            "first_name": "Some",
            "last_name": "Guy",
            "business_name": "Not applicable",
            "address": {
                "line1": "456 Real Fake Dr",
                "city": "Some Place",
                "state": "OR",
                "postal_code": "97501",
                "country_code": "US"
            }
        }
    }
}
```

With the PayPal API, once the invoice is created, I can request (read), update, and delete that invoice.

Operations done behind the scenes in JavaScript, such as the request for the weather data, are referred to as asynchronous. Asynchronous operations are operations that take place in the background without interrupting the main transmission.

In the case of JavaScript asynchronous operations, the "main transmission" would be the display of the web browser. For example, a news web page might include a sidebar with real-time weather data. While you're reading your news article, code in the background could asynchronously update the weather display every 60 seconds. This operation would not require the page to reload, nor would it interrupt your page scrolling to read your article. The only thing on the page to change would be the sidebar with the weather data.

The asynchronous (background) operations of JavaScript are referred to as AJAX. AJAX stands for Asynchronous JavaScript and XML. When we are making behind-the-scenes requests for JSON, this would technically be Asynchronous JavaScript and JSON (AJAJ). However, the term "AJAX" has been used for so long that it has become less of an acronym and more of a word to describe *any* asynchronous operations in JavaScript. Here in this book and elsewhere, you will see the term AJAX used to describe Asynchronous JavaScript and JSON. This is not done in error.

Let's take a look at how we can achieve AJAX with JSON and the JavaScript XMLHttpRequest.

The JavaScript XMLHttpRequest

Though the JavaScript `XMLHttpRequest` sounds like it has to do with XML, we use it for making HTTP requests. During the time it was named with XML in it, XML was the star data interchange format for making these types of requests. However, `XMLHttpRequest` *is not* restricted to XML. We use it to request JSON despite its name.

Earlier, I began several phrases with "Code that fetches." The JavaScript `XMLHttpRequest` is code that fetches a resource. This phraseology is common when talking about HTTP requests, though in reality the code isn't chasing through cyberspace like a dog fetching a ball. The code sits where it is and politely asks for the resource to be delivered.

If we return to the restaurant example, we can imagine the JavaScript code sitting at a restaurant table. The JavaScript code doesn't go to the kitchen to request JSON, nor does it yell across the restaurant. There is protocol in a restaurant. That protocol requires you to summon a waiter who writes down your order and carries it to the kitchen.

There is also protocol that allows code to send requests to web servers that may be hundreds or thousands of miles away. The very foundation of data communication that allows us to visit our favorite websites is based on a protocol called *HyperText Transfer Protocol (HTTP)*. When we type *http://www.cutelittlekittens.com* into our Internet browser, we are using the HyperText Transfer Protocol to make a request for a resource. In the case of the cute kittens website, that resource is an HTML page with cute kitten images embedded into it. Code that needs to make a request for a JSON resource uses the same protocol (HTTP).

In JavaScript, the code that uses the protocol to make this request is the `XMLHttpRequest`. JavaScript is an object-oriented language, so naturally the `XMLHttpRequest` is an object. Once it is created by using the syntax `new XmlHttpRequest()` (Example 6-3), and assigned to a variable, it has functions that can be called to request resources from a location.

Example 6-3. A JavaScript XMLHttpRequest object

```
var myXmlHttpRequest = new XMLHttpRequest();
```

The `XMLHttpRequest` is an object, and Example 6-3 shows the creation of a new `XMLHttpRequest` object. Even if you don't know JavaScript, if you've read the book up to this point, your knowledge of JSON will help you visualize a JavaScript object. After all, JSON is based on the literal notation of JavaScript objects.

We say that a JavaScript object has properties. These "properties" are simply name-value pairs. The properties of the `XMLHttpRequest` are named `onreadystatechange`, readyState, response, responseText, responseType, responseXML, status, status Text, timeout, ontimeout, upload, and withCredentials. Note the inconsistency on the casing of these properties. Some use camelCase and others are all lowercase. This may cause hairpulling in your future if you decide to write your own XMLHttpRequest code, as you will not only need to remember what the properties are called, but the different casing.

One of the key differences between a typical object in programming and a JSON object is that JSON lacks executable instructions. JSON is composed only of properties because it is meant for data interchange. A typical object in programming will also include functions (or methods). For example, I can describe my shoes in JSON with name-value pairs such as: "color": "pink" and "brand": "crocs". What I cannot do in JSON is give life to those shoes, by calling a function (or method) such as shoe.walk().

The available functions of the XMLHttpRequest that we are most interested in are:

- open(*method, url, async* (optional), *user* (optional), *password* (optional))
- send()

The available properties of the XMLHttpRequest that we are most interested in are:

onreadystatechange
    Has a value of a function that we can define in our code.

readyState
    Returns a value ranging from 0–4 that represents a status code.

status
    Returns the HTTP status code (like 200 for success).

responseText
    When the response is successful, this will contain the body of the response as text (JSON if this is what we are requesting).

For those of you not familiar with JavaScript, here is a mind-bender: a property can have a function for a value. This is possible in JavaScript because a function is an object. An object is a type of data, and therefore can be assigned to a variable (property), modified, and passed around. In the programming world, these are called first-class functions. The onreadystatechange property has a value of a function.

Example 6-4 creates a new XMLHttpRequest object and gets JSON from the Open-WeatherMap API.

Example 6-4. A new XMLHttpRequest object

```
var myXMLHttpRequest = new XMLHttpRequest();
var url = "http://api.openweathermap.org/data/2.5/weather?lat=35&lon=139";

myXMLHttpRequest.onreadystatechange = function() {
    if (myXMLHttpRequest.readyState === 4 && myXMLHttpRequest.status === 200) {
        var myObject = JSON.parse(myXMLHttpRequest.responseText);
        var myJSON = JSON.stringify(myObject);
    }
}
myXMLHttpRequest.open("GET", url, true);
myXMLHttpRequest.send();
```

In the example, on the second line of code I'm creating a variable that contains the URL for a JSON resource. I then create a function and assign it to the onreadystate change property of myXMLHttpRequest. This function will be executed every time the readyState property changes. In the function, I check to see if the readyState is 4 (code for "done") and that the HTTP status is 200 (code for success). If both of those things are true, I then parse the JSON into a JSON object.

Two terms that you will often hear about when JSON is turned into text from an object and then from an object back into text are *serialization* and *deserialization*. Serialization is the act of converting the object into text. Deserialization is the act of converting the text back into an object.

In Example 6-5, the JavaScript is deserializing with JSON.parse(). In the response Text, the JSON is simply text as a data interchange format. Once it is parsed by JSON.parse(), it is no longer JSON, but a JavaScript object.

Example 6-5. Deserialization

```
var myJSON = JSON.parse(myXMLHttpRequest.responseText);
```

This deserialization with JSON.parse() is necessary because the JSON is not yet an object. Remember that JSON stands for JavaScript Object *Notation*. While it is in its JSON form, it is a literal representation of an object in the form of text. In order for JSON to become a real object, it must be deserialized. In JavaScript, we can also serialize the JSON with JSON.stringify().

In Example 6-6, the myObject variable gets the deserialized JSON. This is now an object. The myJSON variable gets the serialized object. This is now JSON.

Example 6-6. Object deserialized and then serialized

```
// the JSON response deserialized
var myObject = JSON.parse(myXMLHttpRequest.responseText);

// The object serialized
var myJSON = JSON.stringify(myObject);
```

Finally, the last two lines in my example are setting up the request and then sending it via the HTTP protocol (Example 6-7).

Example 6-7. The request for JSON is set up and sent

```
myXMLHttpRequest.open("GET", url, true);
myXMLHttpRequest.send();
```

You may find it strange that the code that handles the JSON response appears before the request is sent. I even talked about it before I talked about the request being set up and sent. The function value of the onreadystatechange property is an EventHandler. The underlying JavaScript engine (not my code) has logic to access the properties value (my function) every time the ready state changes. The ready states from 0–4 are:

0 for UNSENT
> The state before the open() function has been executed.

1 for OPENED
> The state after the open() function has been executed but before send() has been executed.

2 for HEADERS_RECEIVED
> The state after the send() function has been executed and headers and status are available.

3 for LOADING
> The headers have been received but the response text is still being retrieved.

4 for DONE
> Complete; the full message with headers and body has been received.

> Dealing with status codes for ready states may seem confusing. In Chapter 7, we will see how the XMLHttpRequest can be simplified with jQuery. With jQuery, we can get JSON with a simple getJSON() function, and deal with status in a more human-readable way: done(), fail(), always().

In my example, I used a URL that belongs to the OpenWeatherMap API. This is a web service that provides weather data through an API. The API has URLs for both XML and JSON resources for a variety of weather data. My example showed how I requested and received JSON from this API on the client side with JavaScript. However, Internet browsers have rules about sharing for security purposes. The same-origin policy states that a website should only have these sort of background requests with sites on the same domain. This is to protect users because unless they know what Internet browser developer tools are, they can't *see* these requests happening.

The code I shared in my example could be executed in a script on a site with the URL *http://www.mycoolsite.com*. This is the origin domain because it is the URL of the original request. The URL for the API is:

> *http://api.openweathermap.org/data/2.5/weather?lat=35&lon=139*

The domain *http://api.openweathermap.org* does not match the origin domain of *http://www.mycoolsite.com*. This clearly violates the same-origin policy. This background request and response is only made possible by some hoops that the makers of the OpenWeatherMap API jumped through. Let's take a look at these hoops and loopholes to see how behind-the-scenes requests with public APIs are made possible.

Relationship Woes and Rules About Sharing

I realize I left you on a cliffhanger back there. I just showed you some code that does work, but violates same-origin Internet browser rules. It shouldn't work, but it does, only because of a hoop that the makers of the OpenWeatherMap API jumped through. Sounds like a bad soap opera, where two people can't make up their minds what their relationship is. Will the browser allow the request to the public web API? Stay tuned.

Cross-Origin Resource Sharing (CORS)

Some web developers can go years writing JavaScript AJAX code that makes requests from public web APIs without ever running into same-origin policies. This is because most public APIs have implemented CORS on their own servers. The server supplies some extra properties in the response header prefixed with `Access-Control-Allow` (Example 6-8).

Example 6-8. The Access-Control-Allow headers from the OpenWeatherMap API response for the resource at http://api.openweathermap.org/data/2.5/weather? lat=35&lon=139

```
Access-Control-Allow-Credentials:true
Access-Control-Allow-Methods:GET, POST
Access-Control-Allow-Origin:*
```

These headers define whether credentials are allowed, which of the HTTP methods are allowed (GET, POST, PUT, DELETE, HEAD, OPTIONS, TRACE, CONNECT), and most importantly, which origin domains are allowed. In the example, the asterisk (*) is supplied. This is a wildcard that says any origin domain is allowed.

CORS makes it possible for sites like OpenWeatherMap to share their data in a way that allows users to include it in AJAX interactions on the client side. Additionally, CORS can be used to disallow websites from doing mischievous things with an API such as CSRF. If you remember the example from Chapter 5, a bad guy was able to link to JSON in a <script> tag and exploit the trust of a banking site. A security measure that the bank could put in place is to implement CORS and include the headers shown in Example 6-9 in its response.

Example 6-9. CORS used as a security measure

```
Access-Control-Allow-Methods:POST
Access-Control-Allow-Origin:http://www.somebank.com
```

In the example, POST is the only allowed method. If someone tried to request this resource from a URL in a <script> tag (using the GET method), the browser will not allow it. Additionally, by specifying the URL of the origin site for the bank, the Internet browser will deny access to any website other than *http://www.somebank.com*.

Implementing CORS is not always an option, and JSON is not always hosted by a full-fledged web API. Perhaps you have two sites with two different domains (*http://domainone.com* and *http://domaintwo.com*) and you want to share a JSON file from *http://domainone.com* to *http://domaintwo.com*. This is where JSON-P comes in.

JSON-P

JSON-P stands for JSON with padding. I mentioned in Chapter 5 that <script> tags are exempt from same-origin policies. JSON-P uses this exemption to request JSON from servers without the same origin.

JSON-P is not as ideal as CORS, since it is classified as a workaround (CORS is the preferred method, as it is a standard). However, when push comes to shove, sometimes a workaround like this is needed. You need a relationship between *http://domainone.com* and *http://domaintwo.com*, and the browser rules about sharing can make this frustrating when CORS is not an option.

The "padding" in JSON-P is very simple. It's JavaScript added to the JSON document. See Example 6-10.

Example 6-10. JSON with padding (JSON-P)

```
getTheAnimal(
    {
        "animal": "cat"
    }
);
```

The JavaScript "padding" in this JSON document is a call to a function with the JSON supplied as a parameter. Function parameters provide a way to pass data into the function. For example, if I wanted a function that added two numbers together, I would need a way to pass those two numbers into the function.

This function is defined in our client-side code, in our JavaScript (Example 6-11).

Example 6-11. The function declared in our JavaScript

```
function getTheAnimal(data) {
    var myAnimal = data.animal; // will be "cat"
}
```

After the function is declared in the JavaScript, some setup is required. This is the part of JSON-P that takes advantage of the <script> tag exemption from the same-origin policy. See Example 6-12.

Example 6-12. The <script> tag is created and dynamically appended to the HTML document after the <head> tag

```
var script = document.createElement("script");
script.type = "text/javascript";
script.src = "http://notarealdomain.com/animal.json";
document.getElementsByTagName('head')[0].appendChild(script);
```

For servers implementing JSON-P, it is also customary to allow the user to decide what the function should be named. This is usually passed in via the URL as a query string parameter. See Example 6-13.

Example 6-13. A name for the function communicated to the server via the query string

```
script.src = "http://notarealdomain.com/animal.json?callback=getThing";
```

The server would receive my function name in the callback and generate the padding dynamically in the JSON file. See Example 6-14.

Example 6-14. A dynamically named function in the JSON padding

```
getThing(
    {
        "animal": "cat"
    }
);
```

JSON-P still requires effort on the server side, as the JSON resource must contain the JavaScript padding. Both CORS and JSON-P require an effort on the server side. Therefore, a cross-domain `XMLHttpRequest` by a client is dependent on the server of the JSON resource for success.

Key Terms and Concepts

This chapter covered the following key terms:

Web API
> A set of instructions and standards for interacting with a service over HTTP.

`XMLHttpRequest`
> A JavaScript object, primarily used in AJAX programming, that retrieves data from a URL without reloading the page.

HyperText Transfer Protocol (HTTP)
> The protocol that is the very foundation of data communication for the World Wide Web.

Serialization
> The act of converting the object into text.

Deserialization
> The act of converting the serialized text back into an object.

Same-origin policy
> The Internet browser requires scripts to originate from the same domain for security.

Cross-origin resource sharing (CORS)
> Allows resources (e.g., a JSON document) to be requested from another domain outside of the domain of the requestor by defining permission in the response headers.

JSON with padding (JSON-P)
> Uses the `<script>` tag exemption from the same-origin policy to request JSON from servers without the same origin.

We also discussed these key concepts:

- The relationship between the JavaScript `XMLHttpRequest` and a web API is a client–server relationship.
- `XMLHttpRequest` isn't just for XML. We use it to request JSON resources as well.
- A website caters to humans, and a web API caters to code. Both serve resources over HTTP.
- The same-origin policy can cause relationship woes for client–server interactions between JavaScript and a JSON resource.
- A cross-domain `XMLHttpRequest` by a client is dependent on the server of the JSON resource for success.

CHAPTER 7

JSON and Client-Side Frameworks

In Chapter 6, we took a look at a client–server relationship between the web browser and a web API. In this chapter, we will zoom the lens to the client side of that relationship, and see how some client-side frameworks are supporting or leveraging JSON.

Let's take a quick look at what a framework is, for those that are not familiar with the concept. In the physical world, "framework" can be used to describe an essential supporting structure, or an underlying structure. In computing, a framework is not an underlying structure. It is a structure that sits on a layer above software or a programming language to provide support to the developers.

A framework in computing is a supporting structure, but not in a way that can be related to the beams of a building. If the JavaScript language were a house, a JavaScript framework would not be the supporting structure of that building. In fact, you can build a very strong house without a JavaScript framework.

If we were in the business of building houses with JavaScript, a JavaScript framework would be like ordering a prefabricated house that already contains plumbing and wiring for electricity. With our prefabricated houses, we could focus on creating whatever type of kitchen sink we wanted and running water would just be a matter of connecting the sink to the plumbing. We could focus on installing nice cabinetry and beautiful granite countertops. In essence, our JavaScript framework would allow us to save time and focus on building features.

This time-saving and focus-inducing framework is known in computer science as an abstraction tool. For those not familiar with the concept of abstraction, it may elicit images of Picasso's art with strange faces made from shapes. Abstraction is not complex art, but a technique for dealing with complex systems.

If you were tasked with building a spaceship and you had no experience in rocket science, where would you start? Most of us would say, "Clearly I'm not the best person for this job," but what if you had no choice? You could stare right into the face of that complex task and feel like it is impossible. You could panic and lock yourself into a room. Or, you could use abstraction.

With abstraction, you focus on one piece of the whole puzzle at a time. We break the task of building a spaceship into all of its essential pieces, such as supporting human life on the ship or launching the ship into outer space. We focus on each part of the complex system until the system is whole.

An abstraction tool is any tool that facilitates abstraction. A JavaScript framework facilitates abstraction with prefabricated libraries that have already dealt with complexities in the system. Not that we can build a real spaceship out of a JavaScript framework, but if we could that framework might contain a ship that can already launch into space. This would allow the ship builders to focus on how they are going to support human life inside the ship.

There are many (>50) JavaScript frameworks available today. Oftentimes they are referred to as JavaScript libraries or tool kits. Each of them creates a layer between the complex systems and your task at hand. Many of them allow for easy manipulation of the HTML Document Object Model, and others are focused on building full-fledged client-side web applications.

Let's take a look at some JavaScript frameworks and their relationship with JSON.

jQuery and JSON

jQuery (*http://jquery.com/*) is an abstraction tool that allows developers to focus on building features by catering to manipulation of the HTML Document Object Model (DOM). The is a convention for interacting with the HTML page. In this model, the underlying HTML is treated as an object and a set of nodes that can be enumerated, accessed, and manipulated.

Manipulation of the DOM in JavaScript is possible without the jQuery framework. However, there are some things developers routinely need to do with the DOM that take several lines of code. For example, a common thing to do with the DOM is hide an HTML element. Let's say I have a button that I want hidden (Example 7-1).

Example 7-1. An HTML button that displays in a web browser with the text "My Button"

```
<button id="myButton">My Button</button>
```

As shown in Example 7-2, to achieve the goal of hiding the button in JavaScript, I must call the function getElementById(*id*) on the HTML document object, then set the style.display property to "none".

Example 7-2. This line of JavaScript will hide the HTML button with the id "myButton"; it will not display in the browser

```
document.getElementRyId("myButton").style.display = "none";
```

jQuery achieves the same goal with less than half the characters in code (Example 7-3).

Example 7-3. This line of jQuery will hide the HTML button with the id "myButton"; it will not display in the browser

```
$("#myButton").hide();
```

Having to type less than half the characters to achieve the same goal saves on production time. In addition to saving time, jQuery also deals with Internet browser compatibility issues. For example, in Chapter 5, I brought up JSON.parse() as a safer alternative to eval() for parsing JSON. In older versions of Internet Explorer, Firefox, and Chrome, JSON.parse() is not supported. This means whatever feature you wrote using JSON.parse() will not work for a small percentage of your users who fail to update their browsers.

jQuery deals with many common version compatibility issues for you, including the mentioned JSON.parse() issue. jQuery has a function for parsing JSON: jQuery.par seJSON. In Example 7-4, JSON is parsed with the JavaScript JSON.parse(). In Example 7-5, JSON is parsed with the built-in jQuery function.

Example 7-4. Parsing JSON in JavaScript with JSON.parse()

```
var myAnimal = JSON.parse('{ "animal" : "cat" }');
```

Example 7-5. Parsing JSON with jQuery using jQuery.parseJSON

```
var myAnimal = jQuery.parseJSON('{ "animal" : "cat" }');
```

In the examples, you can see that the jQuery example doesn't appear to be saving any characters for typing. However, the jQuery.parseJSON() function is doing much more than one line of code. If you look at the function code for this in the jQuery library source, it attempts to use the native JSON.parse() function. If that is not available in the browser (for old versions), it falls back to using new Function(), which is the equivalent of using eval(). Additionally, there is some logic checking for invalid characters, which would be present in a script in an injection attack attempt, in which case an error is thrown.

In addition to `jQuery.parseJSON`, there is a function for making an HTTP request for JSON. If we take a look at our example from Chapter 6, we can see that requesting a resource over HTTP with JavaScript can require a good chunk of code (Example 7-6).

Example 7-6. This example code creates a new XMLHttpRequest object and gets JSON from the OpenWeatherMap API

```
var myXMLHttpRequest = new XMLHttpRequest();
var url = "http://api.openweathermap.org/data/2.5/weather?lat=35&lon=139";

myXMLHttpRequest.onreadystatechange = function() {
    if (myXMLHttpRequest.readyState === 4 && myXMLHttpRequest.status === 200) {
        var myObject = JSON.parse(myXMLHttpRequest.responseText);
        var myJSON = JSON.stringify(myObject);
    }
}
myXMLHttpRequest.open("GET", url, true);
myXMLHttpRequest.send();
```

In jQuery, we can request the JSON resource by writing just a few lines of code (Example 7-7).

Example 7-7. This jQuery code will create a new XMLHttpRequest and retrieve the same JSON resource as the preceding example; this includes deserializing the JSON into a JavaScript object

```
var url = "http://api.openweathermap.org/data/2.5/weather?lat=35&lon=139";
$.getJSON(url, function(data) {
    // do something with weather data
});
```

The jQuery JavaScript framework supports JSON in a way that cuts down on production time for requesting and parsing JSON. This includes parsing JSON in a way that support older versions of Internet browsers. We can say that jQuery *supports* interacting with JSON.

Now let's take a look at AngularJS, a library that *leverages* JavaScript objects and JSON.

AngularJS

The jQuery framework is an abstraction tool that caters to manipulation of the Document Object Model (DOM). The AngularJS framework (*https://angularjs.org/*) is an abstraction tool that caters to single-page applications. *Single-page web applications* are web pages that break away from the traditional multipage approach to create a more seamless application experience.

The traditional multipage web application experience is heavily tied to the human interaction between client and server. The human either types in or clicks a URL that makes a request for a resource with HTTP. This dance between the client and server and the human in a traditional web application involves each step "moving" to a new web page.

Before the Internet grew up into a beast that could handle the massive amounts of multimedia that it does today, most applications for the masses were desktop applications. If you wanted a digital encyclopedia, you installed it on your computer. The application that you interacted with was more or less seamless. When you searched for something in your encyclopedia, there was no URL bar with a page that changed addresses.

Single-page web applications seek to return to that seamless application experience right in your Internet browser. Quite a bit of this is achieved through JavaScript, and our good friend XMLHttpRequest. Instead of the human hopping from resource to resource through URLs and links to URLs, the code in the background handles the resource requests while the human remains on one page.

The AngularJS framework is an abstraction tool that saves the developer from having to build the single-page application from the ground up. The single-page web application is a complex system, and by no means does AngularJS build it for the developer. Instead, it provides a framework based on the model-view-controller (MVC) architectural concept.

AngularJS implements the MVC concept as follows:

Model
    JavaScript objects are the data model.

View
    HTML (uses syntax for data binding with the model).

Controller
    The JavaScript files that use the AngularJS syntax defining and handling the interactions with the model and the view.

AngularJS can have a steep learning curve, especially for those that have been working with JavaScript and HTML Document Object Model (DOM) manipulations for years. It requires a shift in thinking about how to interact with the DOM. AngularJS seeks to decouple DOM manipulation from application logic.

This decoupling of DOM manipulation can be expressed by comparing how we would achieve the same goal without the AngularJS framework and with it. For example, I need to change a message on a page from the generic "Hello, stranger" (Example 7-8) to a personalized greeting when a user signs in (Example 7-9). In JavaScript, we would achieve this by manipulating the DOM.

Example 7-8. The HTML message when the user is not signed in

```
<h1 id="message">Hello, stranger!</h1>
```

Example 7-9. The JavaScript to change the message if the user is signed in

```
if (signedIn) {
    var message = "Hello, " + userName + "!";
    document.getElementById("message").innerHTML = message;
}
```

In AngularJS, as the HTML is our view, we set it up to prepare for changes in our data model (Example 7-10).

Example 7-10. The HTML view with AngularJS attributes and syntax for data binding

```
<body ng-app="myApp">
    <div id="wrapper" ng-controller="myAppController">
        <h1 id="message">Hello {{ userData.userName }}!</h1>
    </div>
</body>
```

The `"ng-app"` and `"ng-controller"` attributes on the HTML tags (`<body>` and `<div>`) are syntax for setting up the view to support data binding. Data binding is exactly what it sounds like: we are "binding" data to a page through a series of placeholders. The AngularJS syntax uses "handlebars" for these placeholders where data is to be bound. These handlebars are two open curly brackets (`{{`) and two closing curly brackets (`}}`) surrounding syntax for the placeholder (`userData.userName` in Example 7-10).

In Example 7-11, the JavaScript controller with a `userData` object is added to the global scope; this allows the view (the HTML) to use the object for data binding.

Example 7-11. userData object added to global scope

```
angular.module('myApp', [])
  .controller('myAppController', function($scope) {
    $scope.userData = { userName : "Stranger" };
    if(signedIn)
    {
        $scope.userData = { userName : "Bob" };
    }
  });
```

In the AngularJS JavaScript controller file, instead of manipulating the DOM, the data model is manipulated. The data model being manipulated is the userData object. Both the plain JavaScript/HTML example and the Angular example achieve the same functionality. For my simple example, the Angular way might seem like more effort, especially for an abstraction tool. However, when you delve into a complex application such as a page that allows users to perform create, read, update, and delete (CRUD) operations on their user info, the Angular way simplifies development.

Example 7-11 showed a JavaScript object userData for a data model. AngularJS leverages JavaScript objects by using them as the model in the MVC architecture. As we know, JSON is the notation for JavaScript object literals. So where does JSON fit in with AngularJS?

The question to ask is, "Where does our data model come from?" In the example code, my data model was hardcoded into the controller. If we return to the example of a digital encyclopedia, we know that data has to live somewhere. When data is stored, it is usually stored in a database of some sort.

How we get that data into the data model of our single-page web application is up to the developers. In an AngularJS data model, the most common vehicle for getting that data from the database to the data model is with JSON. This is often a JSON resource requested over HTTP, a client–server relationship. AngularJS leverages this relationship for retrieving data models easily with a core AngularJS service: $http.

In Example 7-12, the AngularJS $http is used to get weather data from the OpenWeatherMap API; the JSON is added to the global scope as an object named weatherData. The response appears in Example 7-13.

Example 7-12. Getting weather data from the OpenWeatherMap API

```
angular.module('myApp', [])
  .controller('myAppController', function($scope, $http) {
    $http.get('http://api.openweathermap.org/data/2.5/weather?lat=35&lon=139').
      success(function(data, status, headers, config) {
            $scope.weatherData = data;
      });
  });
```

Example 7-13. The JSON response from the OpenWeatherMap API

```
{
    "coord": {
        "lon": 139,
        "lat": 35
    },
    "sys": {
        "message": 0.0099,
        "country": "JP",
        "sunrise": 1431805135,
        "sunset": 1431855710
    },
    "weather": [
        {
            "id": 800,
            "main": "Clear",
            "description": "sky is clear",
            "icon": "02n"
        }
    ],
    "base": "stations",
    "main": {
        "temp": 291.116,
        "temp_min": 291.116,
        "temp_max": 291.116,
        "pressure": 1020.61,
        "sea_level": 1028.58,
        "grnd_level": 1020.61,
        "humidity": 95
    },
    "wind": {
        "speed": 1.51,
        "deg": 339.501
    },
    "clouds": {
        "all": 8
    },
    "dt": 1431874405,
    "id": 1851632,
```

```
    "name": "Shuzenji",
    "cod": 200
}
```

The JSON from the OpenWeatherMap API is deserialized by the AngularJS $http. After it is added to the global scope as an object named weatherData, it becomes our data model that we can bind to in our HTML view with handlebars syntax.

In Example 7-14, inside the handlebars syntax, the data being bound is the weather description. The weather description is in the weather property, which contains an array of objects, with only one value. I select the value at index 0 with weather[0] and then the property description.

Example 7-14. Binding the weather description

```
<body ng-app="myApp">
    <div id="wrapper" ng-controller="myAppController">
        <div>
            {{ weatherData.weather[0].description }}
        </div>
    </div>
</body>
```

At the time of writing this chapter, the weather was "sky is clear." I could make this single-page application update every 60 seconds to deliver the description of the current weather. The HTTP request would happen behind the scenes, and the data model updating would automatically change the HTML view. The human would not have to initiate this request; this can all take place in the background. Additionally, with the MVC concept, the JavaScript code I write does not have to make the change to the DOM. Updating the data model automatically updates the view.

AngularJS leverages JavaScript Objects and JSON in its model-view-controller architecture. jQuery supports JSON with easy functions for requesting and parsing JSON. Much of the success of a data interchange format hinges on support by those who interchange data. In the client–server relationship of the Web, we can see that JSON is supported both by JavaScript and its powerful abstraction tools. In Chapters 8 and 9, we will see how JSON is supported and used on the server side of that relationship.

Key Terms and Concepts

This chapter covered the following key terms:

Abstraction
> A technique for dealing with complex systems that involves focusing on smaller areas of that system.

Framework
An abstraction tool that saves time and allows for focus on building features.

`jQuery.parseJSON()`
A function that not only uses the `JSON.parse()` function, but uses a fallback for older browsers that doesn't support `JSON.parse()` and handles the security hole of evaluating a string by validating characters.

`jQuery.getJSON()`
Shorthand for the `jquery.ajax()` function and parsing the JSON into a Java-Script object all in one.

Single-page web applications
Web pages that break away from the traditional multipage approach to create a more seamless application experience.

Model-view-controller (MVC)
An architectural pattern that divides an application into three components: the model (data), the view (presentation), and the controller (updates the model and view).

AngularJS
An MVC JavaScript framework that uses JavaScript objects as the data model.

We also discussed these key concepts:

- jQuery is an abstraction tool that *supports* JSON by cutting down on production time for requesting and parsing data. Additionally, it handles browser-version support issues.
- With the AngularJS MVC concept:
  — JSON is the model (or data model).
  — HTML is the view and uses syntax for data binding with the model.
  — Controllers are the Angular JavaScript files and syntax for defining and handling the interactions with the model and the view.
- AngularJS *leverages* JavaScript objects and JSON in its MVC architecture.

CHAPTER 8

JSON and NoSQL

In Chapter 7, we zoomed the lens to the client side in the client–server relationship of the Web. In this chapter, we are going to zoom that lens to the server side to a type of database that not only uses JSON documents to store data, but interfaces with the outside world through a web API.

We live in the "information age" where vast amounts of data and knowledge are easily accessible. We can query for information on a specific subject like "naked mole-rat" on sites like Wikipedia. The information on "naked mole-rat" has to be stored somewhere, and that somewhere is ultimately a database.

If you've worked with a database in the past and are familiar with SQL, you were most likely working with a *relational database*. Relational databases are structured with tables, columns, and rows. Each table is representative of something, such as an account. The table representing an account may have a relationship with a table that represents addresses for accounts. A key in each table, such as a column that contains an account identifier, forms a relationship between the two tables.

To create, manipulate, and query these relational databases, we use *Structured Query Language (SQL)*. With SQL, I can query for columns and rows from one or more tables of the database (Example 8-1).

Example 8-1. A simple SQL query that will return columns and rows for AccountID, FirstName, and LastName from the Account table

```
SELECT accountId, firstName, lastName
FROM Account
```

With the relationships between the tables in a relational database, I may also query columns and rows from multiple tables (Example 8-2).

Example 8-2. A query joining two tables together; this will return columns and rows for first name, last name, street address, and zip code of all accounts and their related addresses

```
SELECT Account.firstName, Account.lastName, Address.street, Address.zip
FROM Account
JOIN Address
ON Account.accountId = Address.accountId
```

The "NoSQL" title given to a database tells us that it is not a relational database. We cannot use SQL to ask the database for columns and rows of tables joined together. What the title does not tell us is *what it is*. It simply says, "I've found an alternative way to store data that is not relational." Naturally, there is more than one "alternative way."

The NoSQL databases out in the world today vary in nature as much as a tiger from an elephant. These types of databases vary in nature because data has different sizes, shapes, and purposes. The creators of these NoSQL databases realized this and thus created homes for data to be stored and retrieved that break away from the traditional relational mold.

One example of a NoSQL database is a *key-value store*. The key-value store models simple data as key-value pairs. If we were to take the English dictionary and make a database out of it, it could fit well in a key-value store. Each word could be a key, and each definition could be a value. This type of database is a great alternative to the overhead of a relational database for simple data structures.

The type of NoSQL database we are going to explore in this chapter is a *document store*. This alternative to a relational database structures data around the concept of a document rather than representing and relating pieces of data as tables. There are currently 20+ different document store databases being used out in the world today, some using XML documents and others JSON documents.

In this chapter, we will take a look at one type of document store database that uses JSON documents to store data. Let's take a look at CouchDB.

The CouchDB Database

As CouchDB (*http://couchdb.apache.org/*) is a NoSQL database, it has a nonrelational way of storing data with JSON documents.

Let's say I need to store account data for customers. With a relational database, account information could quickly span across several tables. If I needed to have more than one address for an account, then a separate address table would be neces-sary to support this one-to-many relationship.

In a relational database, a one-to-many relationship such as an account with multiple addresses must be queried with a join to put the data back together again. Additionally, if I were to query the database for a single account and all of its address records joined, the results would contain multiple rows. Each row would have a repeat of the same account fields, with a different address for each row. Thus, the structure of the data exists inside of the database, but is flattened into columns and rows when queried.

With CouchDB, the relationships within the data do not require the data to be separated for storage and reassembled later for reading. The relationships are expressed within the data, and the structure is maintained as the data moves in and out of the database.

In Example 8-3, the one-to-many relationship of account addresses is represented as objects in an array.

Example 8-3. A JSON document representing an account

```
{
  "firstName": "Bob",
  "lastName": "Barker",
  "age": 91,
  "addresses": [
    {
      "street": "123 fake st",
      "city": "Somewhere",
      "state": "OR",
      "zip": 97520
    },
    {
      "street": "456 fakey ln",
      "city": "Some Place",
      "state": "CA",
      "zip": 96026
    }
  ]
}
```

With the CouchDB document store, when I ask the database for an account, I get a structured document in return. There is no assembly required. This is both convenient and faster.

However, a document store is not a one-size-fits-all solution for data storage. This model can quickly turn troublesome if multiple associations are needed. What if I wanted to have relationships between cities, states, and zip codes for an address? As soon as these relationships are needed, then the relational model would better suit the data, as it would be difficult to express complex relationships within a single document.

Another thing that CouchDB does well is the facilitation of evolving data. Some data evolves over time. For example, in 1990, I could have probably gotten away with these fields for phone numbers in a record for an account:

- Home Phone
- Work Phone
- Fax

Now that we aren't in 1990, we need a field for a mobile phone. The data needs to evolve.

In a relational database, we would need to modify the schema of the address table to support this mobile phone field. We might also decide to get rid of the fields on the account table and move the phone numbers to their own table.

With CouchDB, our data is allowed to evolve without having to modify schema. I could easily represent phone numbers in JSON as an array of objects (Example 8-4), and allow an account to have as many phone records as they truly have.

Example 8-4. An array of phone number objects

```
{
  "phoneNumbers": [
    {
      "description": "home phone",
      "number": "555-555-5555"
    },
    {
      "description": "cell phone",
      "number": "123-456-7890"
    },
    {
      "description": "fax",
      "number": "456-789-1011"
    }
  ]
}
```

If in the future an account gains a new number, we can just add it to the array, as shown in Example 8-5.

Example 8-5. The array of phone number objects gets a new "space phone"

```
{
  "phoneNumbers": [
    {
      "description": "home phone",
      "number": "555-555-5555"
    },
```

```
  {
    "description": "cell phone",
    "number": "123-456-7890"
  },
  {
    "description": "fax",
    "number": "456-789-1011"
  },
  {
    "description": "space phone",
    "number": "932-932-932"
  }
  ]
}
```

Additionally, if we needed a new field on the account record, such as "galaxy," we would just add it to all future records (Example 8-6). No schema modification required.

Example 8-6. The addition of a "galaxy" field to an account record

```
{
  "firstName": "Octavia",
  "lastName": "Wilson",
  "age": 26,
  "addresses": [
    {
      "street": "123 fake st",
      "city": "Somewhere",
      "state": "OR",
      "zip": 97520
    }
  ],
  "galaxy": "Milky Way"
}
```

Data moves in and out of the CouchDB database as JSON documents. The question now is, how do we put data in, and how do we get it out? Couch DB uses HTTP for an API. Let's take a look at the CouchDB API.

The CouchDB API

With CouchDB, the way we ask the database for data is by requesting resources with HTTP. With HTTP, we make requests for resources with a URL. The resource we request from the CouchDB API is a JSON document (application/json).

If I have a database named "accounts" in my locally installed CouchDB, I can use the URL *http://localhost:5984/accounts/* to get information about the database. In Example 8-7, information about the accounts database is returned in JSON format.

Example 8-7. Response from http://localhost:5984/accounts/

```
{
    "db_name": "accounts",
    "doc_count": 3,
    "doc_del_count": 0,
    "update_seq": 7,
    "purge_seq": 0,
    "compact_running": false,
    "disk_size": 28773,
    "data_size": 1248,
    "instance_start_time": "1432493477586600",
    "disk_format_version": 6,
    "committed_update_seq": 7
}
```

Notice the "doc_count" name-value pair. This specifies how many documents are in my database, and there are currently 3. I can query for each document in the database by the unique identifier for each document, with the URL *http://localhost:5984/ accounts/<unique_identifier>*. If I do not know the unique identifiers for my documents, I can use the URL *http://localhost:5984/accounts/_all_docs* to retrieve an array of the row identifiers.

In Example 8-8, the JSON resource at URL *http://localhost:5984/accounts/_all_docs* contains an array of the document identifiers for each document in my database.

Example 8-8. Array of document identifiers

```
{
    "total_rows": 3,
    "offset": 0,
    "rows": [
        {
            "id": "3636fa3c716f9dd4f7407bd6f7000552",
            "key": "3636fa3c716f9dd4f7407bd6f7000552",
            "value": {
                "rev": "1-8a9527cbfc22e28984dfd3a3e6032635"
            }
        },
        {
            "id": "ddc14efcf71396463f53c0f880001538",
            "key": "ddc14efcf71396463f53c0f880001538",
            "value": {
                "rev": "1-3aef6f6ae7fff90dac3ff5d6c4460ceb"
            }
        },
        {
            "id": "ddc14efcf71396463f53c0f8800019ea",
            "key": "ddc14efcf71396463f53c0f8800019ea",
            "value": {
```

```
                "rev": "5-c38761b818edaf9842a63574927b7d38"
            }
        }
    ]
}
```

If I grab the first identifier (3636fa3c716f9dd4f7407bd6f7000552) from this array, I can then structure a URL to make a request for the document (Example 8-9).

Example 8-9. JSON resource representing an account at URL http://localhost:5984/accounts/3636fa3c716f9dd4f7407bd6f7000552

```
{
    "_id": "3636fa3c716f9dd4f7407bd6f7000552",
    "_rev": "1-8a9527cbfc22e28984dfd3a3e6032635",
    "firstName": "Billy",
    "lastName": "Bob",
    "address": {
        "street": "123 another st",
        "city": "Somewhere",
        "state": "OR",
        "zip": "97501"
    },
    "age": 54,
    "gender": "male",
    "famous": false
}
```

We've seen how to request data from a CouchDB database. Now let's take a look at how we deliver data.

If I want to add another account document to my accounts database, I would do so by posting to the URL *http://localhost:5984/accounts/* (see Examples 8-10 and 8-11).

Example 8-10. HTTP headers for request (http://localhost:5984/accounts/) using POST method

```
POST /accounts/ HTTP/1.1
Host: localhost:5984
Content-Type: application/json
Cache-Control: no-cache
```

Example 8-11. HTTP body for request (http://localhost:5984/accounts/) using POST method

```json
{
    "firstName": "Janet",
    "lastName": "Jackson",
    "address": {
        "street": "456 Fakey Fake st",
        "city": "Somewhere",
        "state": "CA",
        "zip": "96520"
    },
    "age": 54,
    "gender": "female",
    "famous": true
}
```

 If you use Chrome as your Internet browser, check out "Postman" in the Chrome Web Store. Postman gives you a simple interface for building up and testing HTTP requests to APIs with all the HTTP methods (GET, POST, PUT, DELETE, etc.). In addition, Postman saves a history of your requests, so you can test the same requests over and over without having to re-create them.

After the HTTP request is successful, the CouchDB API will deliver a response message in JSON format that includes the newly generated identifier for the document (Example 8-12).

Example 8-12. The JSON response from http://localhost:5984/accounts/

```json
{
    "ok": true,
    "id": "3636fa3c716f9dd4f7407bd6f700076c",
    "rev": "1-363f3b4bf90183781d08fe22487f3c90"
}
```

I may now form a URL using the new unique identifier to request the JSON document from the accounts database (Example 8-13).

Example 8-13. Resource at URL http://localhost:5984/accounts/3636fa3c716f9dd4f7407bd6f700076c

```
{
    "_id": "3636fa3c716f9dd4f7407bd6f700076c",
    "_rev": "1-363f3b4bf90183781d08fe22487f3c90",
    "firstName": "Janet",
    "lastName": "Jackson",
    "address": {
        "street": "456 Fakey Fake st",
        "city": "Somewhere",
        "state": "CA",
        "zip": "96520"
    },
    "age": 54,
    "gender": "female",
    "famous": true
}
```

If I want to update my new JSON document, I can simply include the "_id" and "_rev" name-value pairs in the body of my request and POST to the URL of the resource. For example, if I wanted to update Janet Jackson's age to 55, I would send the same document in the last example with the updated age. The API will then respond with a JSON status document that includes the updated "rev" name-value pair (see Example 8-14).

Example 8-14. Response after posting the updated JSON document to http://localhost:5984/accounts/3636fa3c716f9dd4f7407bd6f700076c

```
{
    "ok": true,
    "id": "3636fa3c716f9dd4f7407bd6f700076c",
    "rev": "3-29ede949ceed9df62bd7caecb095bffe"
}
```

If I want to delete a document, I use the HTTP DELETE method and pass the revision identifier into the URL as a query string parameter (Example 8-15).

Example 8-15. "rev" is communicated as a query string parameter

```
http://localhost:5984/accounts/3636fa3c716f9dd4f7407bd6f700076c?
    rev=3-29ede949ceed9df62bd7caecb095bffe
```

If I request the resource at URL *http://localhost:5984/accounts/* once more, it will now show that there are four documents (Example 8-16).

*Example 8-16. JSON document at URL http://localhost:5984/accounts/; the "doc_count"
name-value pair now has a value of 4*

```json
{
    "db_name": "accounts",
    "doc_count": 4,
    "doc_del_count": 0,
    "update_seq": 8,
    "purge_seq": 0,
    "compact_running": false,
    "disk_size": 32869,
    "data_size": 1560,
    "instance_start_time": "1432493477586600",
    "disk_format_version": 6,
    "committed_update_seq": 8
}
```

These examples showed how we can view and create the JSON documents that are
stored in a CouchDB database. If this were all we could do, we would quickly run into
problems. Perhaps I need a list of last names that only includes famous people. In
CouchDB, we can achieve this with "views." See Example 8-17.

Views are how we can restructure and query the data from a CouchDB database. The
views are stored in a JSON document called a design document. The design document specifies the language, and may include multiple views.

*Example 8-17. A CouchDB design document for the accounts database that includes a
view for famous people*

```json
{
    "_id": "_design/lists",
    "_rev": "8-4124de7756277c6a937004a763d6247d",
    "language": "javascript",
    "views": {
        "famous": {
            "map": "function(doc){if(doc.lastName!==null&&doc.famous){emit
            (doc.lastName,null)}}"
        }
    }
}
```

Each view is an object that may contain a map and reduce function. In Example 8-17,
there is only a map function. The map function takes each document as a parameter,
and then the emit() function is called. This essentially transforms the data
(Example 8-18).

Example 8-18. A closer look at the "map" function for the "famous" view

```
function(doc) {
    if (doc.lastName !== null && doc.famous) {
        emit(doc.lastName, null)
    }
}
```

In Example 8-18, the function checks each JSON document in the database to make sure we have a last name, and that the name-value pair for "famous" is true. The parameters for emit() are key and value, and these will display as name-value pairs in the transformed document result.

I can then request this view as a resource via the URL *http://localhost:5984/accounts/ _design/lists/_view/famous* (see Example 8-19). The structure is /*<db-name>*/_design/ *<design_document_name>*/_view/*<view_name>*/.

Example 8-19. The resource at URL http://localhost:5984/accounts/_design/lists/_view/ famous

```
{
    "total_rows": 2,
    "offset": 0,
    "rows": [
        {
            "id": "ddc14efcf71396463f53c0f880001538",
            "key": "Barker",
            "value": null
        },
        {
            "id": "3636fa3c716f9dd4f7407bd6f700076c",
            "key": "Jackson",
            "value": null
        }
    ]
}
```

In addition to the map step, you may optionally reduce the results. CouchDB has three built-in reduce functions: _count, _sum, and _stats. These are useful after transforming the data with the map step to retrieve statistical information on your data set.

For example, I may want information on how many accounts there are based on gender. I can add a new view to my design document (see Example 8-20).

Example 8-20. The design document with an addition of a "gender_count" view

```
{
    "famous": {
        "map": "function(doc){if(doc.lastName!==null&&doc.famous){emit
        (doc.lastName,null)}}"
    },
    "gender_count": {
        "map": "function(doc){if(doc.gender!==null) emit(doc.gender);}",
        "reduce": "_count"
    }
}
```

In the map step for the `"gender_count"` view, the function is emitting the value from the `"gender"` name-value pair. Without the reduce step, this would produce an array of objects that have the gender value for `"key"` (seeExample 8-21).

Example 8-21. The "gender_count" view after the map step

```
{
    "total_rows": 4,
    "offset": 0,
    "rows": [
        {
            "id": "3636fa3c716f9dd4f7407bd6f700076c",
            "key": "female",
            "value": null
        },
        {
            "id": "ddc14efcf71396463f53c0f8800019ea",
            "key": "female",
            "value": null
        },
        {
            "id": "3636fa3c716f9dd4f7407bd6f7000552",
            "key": "male",
            "value": null
        },
        {
            "id": "ddc14efcf71396463f53c0f880001538",
            "key": "male",
            "value": null
        }
    ]
}
```

After the reduce step with the built-in `"_count"` function, we get a result that provides a count of all the records (see Example 8-22).

Example 8-22. Resource at URL http://localhost:5984/accounts/_design/lists/_view/gender_count

```
{
    "rows": [
        {
            "key": null,
            "value": 4
        }
    ]
}
```

What we are looking for is a count for each unique gender, so we need to pass in the *group* flag to group the results by key. To achieve this, we add a query string parameter *?group=true* to the URL (see Example 8-23).

Example 8-23. Resource at URL http://localhost:5984/accounts/_design/lists/_view/gender_count?group=true

```
{
    "rows": [
        {
            "key": "female",
            "value": 2
        },
        {
            "key": "male",
            "value": 2
        }
    ]
}
```

With the CouchDB API, we can create any number of design documents and views for a database. Each of the views within the design documents optionally contain a map and reduce function to transform the data. We can then create our custom set of URL resources for transformed data sets from our stored JSON documents. Essentially, we can build our own custom API for our data with the CouchDB API.

Key Terms and Concepts

This chapter covered the following key terms:

Relational Database
    A type of database that is structured to recognize relationships in the stored data.

NoSQL Database
    A type of database that is *not* structured on relationships in the stored data.

CouchDB
> A document store type of NoSQL database that stores data in the form of JSON documents.

We also discussed these key concepts:

- In a relational database, there are usually tables, columns, and rows, and relationships between each of those tables, columns, and rows. There are primary keys and foreign keys.
- There are many types of NoSQL databases that break away from the relational model.

We also discussed CouchDB. Here are some key points to remember:

- It is a document store type of NoSQL database.
- It stores and manages JSON documents.
- It maintains the structure of the data as it is stored and retrieved.
- It uses an HTTP API for accessing data as JSON document resources.
- It uses JavaScript as its query language with the map and reduce functions for views that can be accessed through the HTTP API.

CHAPTER 9

JSON on the Server Side

When we talk about web client–server relationships, we can categorize technologies as client side or server side:

- On the client side, we have HTML, CSS, and JavaScript.
- On the server side, there is PHP, ASP.NET, Node.js, Ruby on Rails, Java, Go, and many, many more.

As a web client, we send requests for resources to a server using HTTP. The server responds with a document, such as HTML or JSON. When that document is a JSON document, the server side code must handle the creation of it.

In addition to *serving* a JSON document, a server may *receive* a JSON document. We saw this in Chapter 8 when we used HTTP to post a JSON document to the CouchDB web API. When a document is received, the server-side code must handle the parsing of that document.

In previous chapters, we discussed how JavaScript can make behind-the-scenes HTTP requests for JSON resources to web APIs. It's easy to think of JavaScript playing this role because it is categorized as "client side." However, JavaScript isn't the only language that can make HTTP requests for JSON resources. HTTP requests can also be made by a server-side web framework.

In the scenario where JSON is requested by a server-side technology, its role becomes the client. Here are some example scenarios where HTTP requests are made by server-side web framework code:

- Using a web API for data to populate dynamic pages of a website. This could be a public third-party web API or your own private web API such as CouchDB.
- Integrating a payment gateway into checkout code for an ecommerce website by communicating with a web API.

- Using a web API for retrieving real-time shipping costs for shipping to a specific address.

In this chapter, we will be examining JSON's role on the server side. A server-side web framework or scripting language produces dynamic web pages. When a request is made for a resource, the server creates the resource with some programming logic.

Serializing, Deserializing, and Requesting JSON

The success of a data interchange format on the Web requires support on both the client and server side. If we were to have support on the client side, but not the server side, JSON would be dead in the water. Fortunately, JSON is widely supported by most server-side web frameworks or scripting languages. If they do not have built-in support for serializing and deserializing JSON, it is likely that a library or extension exists to support it.

 As you'll recall from Chapter 6, serialization is the act of converting the object into text. Deserialization is the act of converting the text back into an object.

Let's take a look how JSON can be serialized, deserialized, and requested server side.

ASP.NET

ASP.NET is a server-side web framework developed by Microsoft. Originally, web development with this framework was achieved solely with Web Forms, a GUI state-driven model. However, it now includes several extensions that allow for development with different models, such as ASP.NET MVC (a model-view-controller architecture), and ASP.NET web API (an architecture for building HTTP web APIs for Web Services).

Additionally, ASP.NET uses Common Language Runtime (CLR), which allows developers to write their code in any CLR-supported language such as C#, F#, Visual Basic .NET (VB.NET), and many more. In this section, I will be writing all examples in C#.

Unlike JavaScript, ASP.NET does not easily parse JSON. To parse JSON, we must choose a third-party ASP.NET library and bring it into our project. At the time this book is written, the most popular library is Json.NET, an open source JSON framework by Newtonsoft.

Let's take a look at how we can serialize and deserialize JSON with the Json.NET library.

Serializing JSON

With ASP.NET and Json.NET, we can quickly serialize our ASP.NET objects into JSON. First, I need an object to work with. For this example, we will create an account object with the same structure that we used in Chapter 8 (see Example 9-1).

Example 9-1. A CustomerAccount object in ASP.NET C#

```
public class CustomerAccount
{
    public string firstName { get; set; }
    public string lastName { get; set; }
    public string phone { get; set; }
    public Address[] addresses { get; set; }
    public bool famous { get; set; }
}

public class Address
{
    public string street { get; set; }
    public string city { get; set; }
    public string state { get; set; }
    public int zip { get; set; }
}
```

Now that we have a class representing our object, let's create a new object, for Bob Barker's account. On the very last line, we will serialize this object to JSON using the Json.NET library (see Examples 9-2 and 9-3).

Example 9-2. A new object for Bob Barker's account in C#; in the last line, we serialize this object to JSON

```
CustomerAccount bobsAccount = new CustomerAccount();
bobsAccount.firstName = "Bob";
bobsAccount.lastName = "Barker";
bobsAccount.phone = "555-555-5555";

Address[] addresses;
addresses = new Address[2];

Address bobsAddress1 = new Address();
bobsAddress1.state = "123 fakey st";
bobsAddress1.city = "Somewhere";
bobsAddress1.state = "CA";
bobsAddress1.zip = 96520;

addresses[0] = bobsAddress1;

Address bobsAddress2 = new Address();
bobsAddress2.state = "456 fake dr";
```

```
bobsAddress2.city = "Some Place";
bobsAddress2.state = "CA";
bobsAddress2.zip = 96538;

addresses[1] = bobsAddress2;

bobsAccount.addresses = addresses;
bobsAccount.famous = true;

string json = JsonConvert.SerializeObject(bobsAccount);
```

Example 9-3. The resulting JSON from the serialization of the ASP.NET CustomerAccount object

```
{
    "firstName": "Bob",
    "lastName": "Barker",
    "phone": "555-555-5555",
    "addresses": [
        {
            "street": null,
            "city": "Somewhere",
            "state": "CA",
            "zip": 96520
        },
        {
            "street": null,
            "city": "Some Place",
            "state": "CA",
            "zip": 96538
        }
    ],
    "famous": true
}
```

Deserializing JSON

We can deserialize JSON back into an ASP.NET object with one line of code (Example 9-4).

Example 9-4. The deserialization of the JSON string from the earlier example; it is deserialized to the specified type, "CustomerAccount"

```
CustomerAccount customerAccount =
    JsonConvert.DeserializeObject<CustomerAccount>(json);
```

Json.NET gives us the ability to deserialize our JSON into a specific type of object, such as the `CustomerAccount` object from the example. With this, our data can retain its shape as it moves in and out of the server-side code. However, it is important that our object property names match up with the names of the name-value pairs in our JSON document. Otherwise, deserialization will fail.

Requesting JSON

To make an HTTP request for a resource, I can use the built-in ASP.NET Sys tem.Net.WebClient class. With this class, I can call the DownloadString method to download the requested resource from a specified URL as a string (see Examples 9-5 and 9-6).

Example 9-5. Downloading a JSON address document as a string from my local CouchDB addresses database

```
using(var webClient = new WebClient())
{
    string json = webClient.DownloadString("3636fa3c716f9dd4f7407bd6f700076c");
}
```

Example 9-6. The JSON resource at the URL http://localhost:5984/accounts/ 3636fa3c716f9dd4f740/bd6f700076c

```
{
    "_id": "3636fa3c716f9dd4f7407bd6f700076c",
    "_rev": "2-e04207c11104e06b3a8f030f14c35580",
    "address": {
        "street": "456 Fakey Fake st",
        "city": "Somewhere",
        "state": "CA",
        "zip": "96520"
    },
    "age": 54,
    "gender": "female",
    "famous": true,
    "firstName": "Janet",
    "lastName": "Jackson"
}
```

Once we have our JSON resource as a string, we can then deserialize it into a desired ASP.NET object using the Json.NET DeserializeObject method (Example 9-7).

Example 9-7. Deserialization of the JSON resource as a string; the fullName variable in the last line of code will evaluate to "Janet Jackson"

```
CustomerAccount customerAccount;
using (var webClient = new WebClient())
{
    string json = webClient.DownloadString(
        "http://localhost:5984/accounts/3636fa3c716f9dd4f7407bd6f700076c");
    customerAccount = JsonConvert.DeserializeObject<CustomerAccount>(json);
}

string fullName = customerAccount.firstName + " " + customerAccount.lastName;
```

In these examples, we can see that the structure of the JSON object makes it friendly for ASP.NET objects. So long as the properties of the ASP.NET object and the names of the name-value pairs of the JSON match up, serializing and deserializing JSON in this web framework is simple.

PHP

PHP is a server-side scripting language used to make dynamic web pages. The PHP code can be embedded directly into HTML documents (see Example 9-8).

Example 9-8. This HTML page will display a header (<h1>) tag with the text "Hello, World"

```
<!DOCTYPE html>
<html>
    <head>
        <meta charset="UTF-8">
        <title>Hello, World</title>
    </head>
    <body>
        <h1>
        <?php
            echo "Hello, World";
        ?>
        </h1>
    </body>
</html>
```

Additionally, PHP includes the object data type. Objects are defined with a class (see Example 9-9).

Example 9-9. A PHP class representing a cat

```php
class Cat
{
    public $name;
    public $breed;
    public $age;
    public $declawed;
}
```

When a class is instantiated, an object is created. The object can then be used in programming logic (Example 9-10).

Example 9-10. The class is instantiated, and the properties set. An object is created. The last line of code will display "Fluffy Boo."

```php
$cat = new Cat();
$cat->name = "Fluffy Boo";
$cat->breed = "Maine Coon";
$cat->age = 2.5;
$cat->declawed = false;

echo $cat->name;
```

PHP also includes built-in support for serializing and deserializing JSON. PHP refers to this as encoding and decoding JSON. When we encode something, we convert it to a coded (unreadable) form. When we decode something, we convert it back into a readable form. From the perspective of PHP, JSON is in a coded format. Therefore, to serialize JSON, the `json_encode` function is called, and to deserialize JSON, the `json_decode` function is called.

Serializing JSON

In PHP, we can quickly serialize PHP objects with the built-in support for JSON. In this section, we will create a PHP object representing an address, and serialize to JSON.

In Example 9-11, we first create a class representing an account. Then, we create a new instance of the class for Bob Barker's account. An Account object is created. Finally, on the last line, we call the built-in function `json_encode` to serialize the Account object (results shown in Example 9-12).

Example 9-11. Creating and serializing an account

```php
<?php
class Account {
    public $firstName;
    public $lastName;
    public $phone;
    public $gender;
    public $addresses;
    public $famous;
}

class Address {
    public $street;
    public $city;
    public $state;
    public $zip;
}

$address1 = new Address();
$address1->street = "123 fakey st";
$address1->city = "Somewhere";
$address1->state = "CA";
$address1->zip = 96027;

$address2 = new Address();
$address2->street = "456 fake dr";
$address2->city = "Some Place";
$address2->state = "CA";
$address2->zip = 96345;

$account = new Account();
$account->firstName = "Bob";
$account->lastName = "Barker";
$account->gender = "male";
$account->phone = "555-555-5555";
$account->famous = true;
$account->addresses = array ($address1, $address2);

$json = json_encode($account);

?>
```

Example 9-12. The JSON result from json_encode($account)

```
{
    "firstName": "Bob",
    "lastName": "Barker",
    "phone": "555-555-5555",
    "gender": "male",
```

```
    "addresses": [
        {
            "street": "123 fakey st",
            "city": "Somewhere",
            "state": "CA",
            "zip": 96027
        },
        {
            "street": "456 fake dr",
            "city": "Some Place",
            "state": "CA",
            "zip": 96345
        }
    ],
    "famous": true
}
```

Deserializing JSON

To serialize JSON in PHP, we used the built-in json_encode function. To deserialize JSON, we use the json_decode function. Unfortunately, this does not have built-in support for deserializing the JSON to a specified PHP object, such as the Account class. So, we must do a little processing to reshape our data back into the PHP object.

Let's add a new function to the Account object, to load up its properties from a JSON string.

In Example 9-13, the loadFromJSON function accepts a JSON string for a parameter, calls the built-in json_decode function to deserialize to a generic PHP object, and maps the name-value pairs to the Account properties by name in the foreach loop.

Example 9-13. Adding a function to the Account object

```php
class Account {
    public $firstName;
    public $lastName;
    public $phone;
    public $gender;
    public $addresses;
    public $famous;

    public function loadFromJSON($json)
    {
        $object = json_decode($json);
        foreach ($object AS $name => $value)
        {
            $this->{$name} = $value;
        }
    }
}
```

Next, we can create a new `Account` object, and call the new `loadFromJSON` function (Example 9-14).

Example 9-14. Calling our new loadFromJSON function to deserialize the account JSON back into the Account object; the last line will display "Bob Barker"

```php
$json = json_encode($account);

$deserializedAccount = new Account();
$deserializedAccount->loadFromJSON($json);

echo $deserializedAccount->firstName . " " . $deserializedAccount->lastName;
```

Requesting JSON

To make an HTTP request for a resource with PHP, I can use the built-in function `file_get_contents`. This function returns the resource body as a string. We can then deserialize the string to a PHP object (see Examples 9-15 and 9-16).

Example 9-15. Resource at URL http://localhost:5984/accounts/ ddc14efcf71396463f53c0f8800019ea from my local CouchDB API

```json
{
    "_id": "ddc14efcf71396463f53c0f8800019ea",
    "_rev": "6-69fd853972074668f99b88a86aa6a083",
    "address": {
        "street": "123 fakey ln",
        "city": "Some Place",
        "state": "CA",
        "zip": "96037"
    },
    "gender": "female",
    "famous": false,
    "age": 28,
    "firstName": "Mary",
    "lastName": "Thomas"
}
```

Example 9-16. Calling the built-in file_get_contents function to get the account JSON resource from the CouchDB API. Next, a new Account object is created and our loadFromJSON function is called to deserialize. The last line will display "Mary Thomas."

```php
$url = "http://localhost:5984/accounts/3636fa3c716f9dd4f7407bd6f700076c";
$json = file_get_contents($url);

$deserializedAccount = new Account();
$deserializedAccount->loadFromJSON($json);
```

```
echo $deserializedAccount->firstName . " " . $deserializedAccount->lastName;
```

A Smorgasbord of JSON HTTP Requests

In both the PHP and ASP.NET examples, we can see that though JSON is based on the object literal notation of the JavaScript language, the notation translates well to objects of other programming languages. As server-side programming languages are many and diverse, many of them support objects and the data types of JSON. This is ideal, as it allows the structure or "shape" of the data to be maintained as it moves in and out of a system as JSON.

Additionally, the support for JSON on the server side is massive. Most server-side languages (or frameworks) either provide built-in support for JSON serializing/deserializing, or have libraries or modules available. This support for JSON on the server side contributes to its success as a data interchange format.

Let's take a look at a few bite-sized examples of JSON HTTP requests on the server side. In each of these examples, you will see an HTTP request for a JSON resource, the parsing of that resource into an object, and the rendering of a value from a JSON document.

The JSON document in all these examples will be from the OpenWeatherMap API. All the rendering of values will be based on a subset of the JSON resource at *http://api.openweathermap.org/data/2.5/weather?q=London,uk* (see Example 9-17).

Example 9-17. The coordinates object of the JSON resource for weather data from the OpenWeatherMap API; this represents the latitude and longitude of London, UK

```
{
    "coord": {
        "lon": -0.13,
        "lat": 51.51
    }
}
```

Ruby on Rails

Ruby on Rails is a server-side web application framework. It is written in the Ruby programming language and based on the model-view-controller (MVC) architecture.

In Ruby, a gem is a package for installing a program or library. To serialize and deserialize JSON in Ruby on Rails, the JSON ruby gem is required. Once you have the JSON gem installed, parsing JSON is as simple as `JSON.parse()` (Example 9-18).

In Example 9-18, we make an HTTP request to the OpenWeatherMap API and deserialize the JSON into a Ruby Object. Finally, in the last line of the code, we render the longitude (lon) from the coordinates (coord) object of the data.

Example 9-18. HTTP Request to the OpenWeatherMap API

```ruby
require 'net/http'
require 'json'

url = URI.parse('http://api.openweathermap.org/data/2.5/weather?q=London,uk')
request = Net::HTTP::Get.new(url.to_s)
response = Net::HTTP.start(url.host, url.port) {|http|
http.request(request)
}

weatherData = JSON.parse(response.body)

render text: weatherData["coord"]["lon"]
```

Node.js

Node.js is JavaScript on the server side (without an Internet browser), made possible with Google's open source V8 JavaScript engine. With Node.js, you can build server-side applications with JavaScript.

Earlier in this book, we covered JSON with JavaScript on the client side and saw that JSON is deserialized into a JavaScript object with a simple JSON.parse(). The same is true in Node.js, as it *is* JavaScript.

However, we don't use the XMLHttpRequest object in Node.js, as it is a JavaScript object specific to Internet browsers. In Node.js, we can request our JSON (and other types of resources) with a much better named function: get().

In Example 9-19, we make an HTTP request to the OpenWeatherMap API and deserialize the JSON into a JavaScript Object. We then print the longitude (lon) from the coordinates (coord) object of the data with console.log().

Example 9-19. Making an HTTP request to the API and deserializing to a JavaScript object

```javascript
var http = require('http');
http.get({
    host: 'api.openweathermap.org',
    path: '/data/2.5/weather?q=London,uk'
}, function(response) {
    var body = '';
    response.on('data', function(data) {
        body += data;
```

```
    });
    response.on('end', function() {
        var weatherData = JSON.parse(body);
        console.log(weatherData.coord.lon);
    });
});
```

Java

Java is an object-oriented programming language. Java can be run in the web browser as Java applets, or standalone on a machine with the Java Runtime Environment (JRE).

There are many libraries available that support JSON in Java. In this section, I will use the following libraries to get the JSON resource from a URL and deserialize it to an object in Java:

- Apache Commons IO (*https://commons.apache.org/proper/commons-io/*)
- JSON in Java (*http://www.json.org/java/*)

In Example 9-20, we get the JSON resource as a string from the OpenWeatherMap API. After that, we deserialize the JSON string by instantiating a `JSONObject`. We then print the longitude (`lon`) from the coordinates (`coord`) object of the data with `System.out.println()`.

Example 9-20. Deserializing a JSON string with a JSONObject

```
import java.io.IOException;
import java.net.URL;

import org.apache.commons.io.IOUtils;
import org.json.JSONException;
import org.json.JSONObject;

public class HelloWorldApp {

    public static void main(String[] args) throws IOException, JSONException {
        String url = "http://api.openweathermap.org/data/2.5/weather?q=London,uk";
        String json = IOUtils.toString(new URL(url));
        JSONObject weatherData = new JSONObject(json);
        JSONObject coordinates = weatherData.getJSONObject("coord");
        System.out.println(coordinates.get("lon"));
    }

}
```

Key Terms and Concepts

This chapter covered the following key terms:

ASP.NET
> A server-side web framework developed by Microsoft.

PHP
> A server-side scripting language used to make dynamic web pages.

Ruby on Rails
> A server-side web application framework running on Ruby.

Node.js
> JavaScript on the server side running on Google's V8 JavaScript engine.

Java
> An object-oriented programming language.

We also discussed these key concepts:

- On the server side, JSON can be deserialized into an object for use in programming logic and serialized into JSON format from an object.
- JSON has a huge amount of support on *both* the client side and the server side, which makes it a very successful data interchange format for the Web.

CHAPTER 10

Conclusion

From about 6,000 feet, we can see JSON flitting about in the world, carrying data in and out of systems. JSON is great at doing its job as a data interchange format, and we have seen that expressed in this book. However, if you look closely through your binoculars, you can see that JSON is simply staying put in some places.

Despite the phenomena of JSON staying put in some places, this book has mostly ignored the subject. The focus has been on interchanging data between two parties. Essentially, moving data.

JSON can be both a receptacle and a vehicle for data, and it is not bound to a single purpose. We saw that illustrated with the role of JSON in NoSQL. More and more, JSON is making its way into projects and endeavors as a very useful tool. To further illustrate, let's take one last look at a role that JSON plays out in the world today: staying put in one place as a configuration file.

JSON as a Configuration File

In Chapter 9, we explored two server-side web technologies that support parsing JSON. As discussed in that chapter, JSON is widely supported by most server-side web languages (or frameworks). It has become popular to use JSON for storing configuration data due to wide support, ease of parsing on the server, and human readability.

A configuration or settings file is often used in software, so settings may be changed without having to recompile. There are several formats for configuration files, including INI and XML.

Let's take a look at how we could store the same settings information in INI, XML, and JSON format (in Examples 10-1, 10-2, and 10-3, respectively).

Example 10-1. An example of a game settings file in INI format (settings.ini)

```ini
[general]
playIntro=false
mouseSensitivity=0.54

[display]
complexTextures=true
brightness=4.2
widgetsPerFrame=326
mode=windowed

[sound]
volume=1
effects=0.68
```

Example 10-2. An example of a game settings file in XML format (settings.xml)

```xml
<?xml version="1.0" encoding="UTF-8" ?>
<settings>
    <general>
        <playIntro>false</playIntro>
        <mouseSensitivity>0.54</mouseSensitivity>
    </general>
    <display>
        <complexTextures>true</complexTextures>
        <brightness>4.2</brightness>
        <widgetsPerFrame>326</widgetsPerFrame>
    </display>
    <sound>
        <volume>1</volume>
        <effects>0.68</effects>
    </sound>
</settings>
```

Example 10-3. An example of a game settings file in JSON format (settings.json)

```
{
    "general": {
        "playIntro": false,
        "mouseSensitivity": 0.54
    },
    "display": {
        "complexTextures": true,
        "brightness": 4.2,
        "widgetsPerFrame": 326,
        "mode": "windowed"
    },
    "sound": {
        "volume": 1,
        "effects": 0.68
    }
}
```

All three of these formats are human readable. If I wanted to change my sound settings, I could quickly locate this in each of the files and change the numbers. This is what makes them great for configuration files.

Each of these formats has its own pros and cons. The INI file is easier for a human to read since it's lacking the less-than and greater-than symbols of the XML and the curly brackets and double quotes of JSON. The INI is not so great for more complex data, such as nested information or complex lists. XML can accommodate more complex data, but it does not have data types like JSON.

In addition to the pros and cons for each data format, ease of parsing by the language/framework being used is also important to consider. If a JSON parser is already being used heavily by your application, then JSON may be the best fit for your configuration file.

In Chapter 9, we took a brief look at Node.js with JSON on the server side. A good real-world example of JSON as a configuration file is the JavaScript package manager that is the default for Node.js: npm. It is also used by other frameworks such as AngularJS and jQuery.

The npm package manager uses JSON as a configuration file called *package.json*. The *package.json* file contains information specific to each package, such as the name, version, author, contributors, dependencies, scripts, and licensing (see Example 10-4).

Example 10-4. An example package.json file for npm

```
{
  "name": "bobatron",
  "version": "1.0.0",
  "description": "The extraordinary library of Bob.",
  "main": "bob.js",
  "scripts": {
    "prepublish": "coffee -o lib/ -c src/bob.coffee"
  },
  "repository": {
    "type": "git",
    "url": "git://github.com/bobatron/bob.git"
  },
  "keywords": [
    "bob",
    "tron"
  ],
  "author": "Bob Barker <bob.barker@fakemail.com> (http://bob.com/)",
  "license": "BSD-3-Clause",
  "bugs": {
    "url": "https://github.com/bobatron/issues"
  }
}
```

Though JSON is sitting in one place as a configuration file, it is still playing the role of a data interchange format. In the case of a settings file that sits in a directory somewhere, the interchange is happening between the human and the computer. The data is communicated.

The Big Picture

As a configuration file sitting on a server, or a resource being requested by a URL, JSON is doing its job as a data interchange format. We've explored these jobs (or roles) in the chapters of this book. Let's do a big picture recap of how JSON is being used out in the world today.

On the server side, objects can be serialized to the JSON text format, and deserialized back into an object. JSON can also be requested from the server-side code. We saw this in action with both the ASP.NET and PHP examples discussed in Chapter 9.

Additionally, JSON is a text format that can also be used as a document for a document store type of database. We saw this in Chapter 8 with CouchDB. This database was also interfaced with through an HTTP web API.

An HTTP web API provides a request and response system for resources such as HTML and JSON documents. These documents are requested via HTTP with a URL.

We also saw this in Chapter 6 with the OpenWeatherMap API providing weather data as JSON resources.

The JavaScript `XmlHttpRequest` can request a JSON resource from a URL. To use the JSON in the JavaScript code, we must deserialize the JSON to a JavaScript object. This is quickly achieved with the built-in JavaScript `JSON.parse()` function.

From a JavaScript object, to the JSON format, to an object on the server, we can see the data move full circle. Every day data moves in and out of systems around the world, and that data is in an interchange format.

If we again take a look from 6,000 feet, we can see that JSON is not alone as a data interchange format. Some data is being moved around in a comma-separated values (CSV) format, or an Excel format. Both are tabular. Other data is being moved in an XML format, which supports nesting of data.

Data has many formats, and many shapes. Systems that push out and receive data in these formats are diverse. Both the shape of the data and the systems interchanging the data have to be considered when choosing a format for data interchange. As much as this book loves JSON and views it as a fantastic format for data, JSON is not always the answer.

For example, let's say two systems needed to communicate inventory data, and those two systems both stored that information in a tabular format. Would it make sense to convert that tabular data into an object format, serialize to JSON, convert back into an object format, and then back into tabular data again? No, in that case we'd be adding extra steps just for the sake of JSON. A more appropriate format for this data would be a tabular one, such as CSV or tab delimited.

JSON is a popular format for data interchange because many systems are modeling data as objects. The data is often being stored in a relational database. Though the tables of relational databases are tabular, the relationships in the data are broken out into entities that can be seen as objects. Each entity, such as an address, has "fields" that are essentially name-value pairs.

In systems such as an Internet browser, where JavaScript supports object-oriented programming, JSON is ideal for interchanging data. JSON is great in JavaScript for communicating with web APIs and creating AJAX interactions.

In systems such as a server-side web framework that is object oriented, JSON is ideal for interchanging data. JSON shines for data by maintaining its structure as an object literal as it moves in and out of the system.

Like the example in "JSON as a Configuration File" on page 101, the pros and cons must be examined for choosing a format. It all boils down to the right tool for the right job.

Index

Symbols

" " (quotation marks, double)
  enclosing string values in JSON, 17
  in JSON name-value pairs, 9
  in JSON strings, 7
  inside JSON strings, 17
$ (dollar sign), 20
' ' (quotation marks, single)
  in JavaScript object syntax, 9
  JSON strings and, 17
, (comma) in JSON syntax, 8
/ (forward slash), 18
: (colon) in name-value pairs, 7, 8
[ ] (square brackets)
  enclosing arrays in JSON, 22
  in JSON arrays, 8
\ (backslash)
  characters that must be escaped, 18
  escape special characters in strings, 18
  escaping double quotation marks inside
    strings, 18
{ } (curly braces
  enclosing JSON objects, 8
  in AngularJS handlebars syntax, 68

A

abstraction, 64
Access-Control-Allow headers, 57
AJAX, 52
AngularJS, 66-71
  implementation of MVC architecture, 67
    binding data model to HTML view, 71
    controller, 68
    HTML view, 68

    retrieving data models with $http ser-
      vice, 69
    using JavaScript objects as model, 69
Apache Commons IO, 99
application/json MIME type, 11
architectural decisions leading to security holes,
  45
array literals, 14
arrays
  array data type, 21-26
    data types of array values, 24
    index, 22
    multidimensional arrays, 25
  array of phone number objects in CouchDB,
    76
  top-level JSON array, 41
ASP.NET, 40, 88
  deserializing JSON into ASP.NET object, 90
  requesting a JSON resource, 91
  serializing ASP.NET objects into JSON, 89
Asynchronous JavaScript and XML (see AJAX)
asynchronous operations, 52
attributes, 8

B

\b (backspace) character, 18
booleans, 6, 14
  arrays of, 25
  boolean data type, 20
browsers
  compatibility issues, jQuery and, 65
  cross-browser support for JSON.parse(), 44
  JSON as ideal data interchange format, 105
  same-origin policies, 57

JavaScript padding in JSON-P, 59

G
GET method, 42, 58

H
handlebars syntax (AngularJS), 68
HTML
    Document Object Model (DOM), 64
        interacting with, using AngularJS, 67
    in client-side code, 40
    including within JSON, security concerns
        with, 45
    PHP embedded directly into a page, 92
    script tags, 41
HTTP
    Access-Control-Allow headers, 57
    CouchDB API, 77-85
    GET and POST methods, 42
    requesting JSON with ASP.NET, 91
    requesting JSON with PHP, 96
    requests for resources via, 53
    requests made by server-side web frame-
        works, 87
    server-side requests for JSON, miscellane-
        ous, 97
        Java, 99
        Node.js, 98
        Ruby on Rails, 97
    status codes, 54
    web APIs over, 51

I
IDEs (integrated development environments),
    syntax validation with, 10
indexes (array), 22
INI format (configuration files), 101
injection attacks, 43
    architectural decisions and, 46
    cross-site scripting (XSS), 43-45
integrated development environments (IDEs),
    syntax validation with, 10

J
Java, 40
    server-side HTTP requests for JSON, 99
JavaScript, 2
    asynchronous operations, 52

eval() function, 43
    frameworks, 64
    in client-side code, 40
    object literals, 6, 9
    variables, 23
    XMLHttpRequest, 53
jQuery, 56, 64-66
    dealing with browser compatibility issues,
        65
    manipulating the DOM, 64
    requesting a JSON resource over HTTP, 66
jQuery.getJSON() function, 66
jQuery.parseJSON() function, 65
JSON
    about, 1
    AJAX and, 52
    as a configuration file, 101
    current state of, 101
        big picture, 104
    language independence, 2
    libraries supporting JSON in Java, 99
    syntax, 5-12
    terms and concepts, 4
.json file extension, 11
JSON in Java library, 99
JSON Schema
    documentation, 36
    introduction to, 31
    questions answered by, 32
JSON Schema Lint, 36
JSON Schema Validator, 37
JSON-P (JSON with padding), 58
Json.NET framework, 88
JSON.parse() function, 44, 65
    deserialization with, 55
JSON.stringify() function, 55

K
key-value stores, 74

L
literals, 5

M
map functions (CouchDB), 82
media type (JSON), 11
MIME type (JSON), 11
model-view-controller (MVC) architecture, 67

About the Author

Lindsay Bassett has a passion for both writing about and teaching technology. Her online technology courses and books share the same "to-the-point" style that caters to the busy IT professional or student. She distills each subject down to the fundamentals and has a knack for turning dry technical subjects into enjoyable light reading.

Colophon

The animal on the cover of *Introduction to JavaScript Object Notation* is a harbor seal (*Phoca vitulina*), a marine mammal commonly found in temperate and arctic waters along the coastline of North America and Europe. They are "true seals," meaning that they have short front flippers, stout sausage-like bodies, and no external ear flaps.

Each harbor seal can be identified by a unique pattern of spots, and coloration varies: they can be silver, gray, brown, bluish-gray, or tan, with dark or light spots depending on the main color of their coat. The average body length is 6 feet and weight can range from 120 to 370 pounds; females are slightly smaller than males.

While seals may appear clumsy when wriggling themselves onto land (known as "hauling out"), their sleek frame and strong rear flippers make them agile and formidable in the water. Their diet varies seasonally as they move between different feeding grounds, but harbor seals generally eat a variety of fish, squid, crustaceans, and mollusks. They can dive up to 1,500 feet and spend up to 40 minutes underwater, but shallow dives lasting 3–7 minutes are more common.

Harbor seals spend roughly half their time on land—primarily to rest and regulate their temperature, but also for social interaction and giving birth. Seals often have favorite resting and pupping sites, but will abandon the location if it is disturbed too often by humans. For this reason, coastal development near known seal haul-out beaches needs to be carefully considered.

Harbor seal pups are able to swim at birth, and within a few days, can remain underwater for up to two minutes. They are weaned after four to six weeks, but almost double their weight in this time due to the high fat content of their mother's milk.

Many of the animals on O'Reilly covers are endangered; all of them are important to the world. To learn more about how you can help, go to animals.oreilly.com.

The cover image is from *Lydekker's Royal Natural History*. The cover fonts are URW Typewriter and Guardian Sans. The text font is Adobe Minion Pro; the heading font is Adobe Myriad Condensed; and the code font is Dalton Maag's Ubuntu Mono.

Get even more for your money.

Join the O'Reilly Community, and register the O'Reilly books you own. It's free, and you'll get:

- $4.99 ebook upgrade offer
- 40% upgrade offer on O'Reilly print books
- Membership discounts on books and events
- Free lifetime updates to ebooks and videos
- Multiple ebook formats, DRM FREE
- Participation in the O'Reilly community
- Newsletters
- Account management
- 100% Satisfaction Guarantee

Signing up is easy:

1. Go to: oreilly.com/go/register
2. Create an O'Reilly login.
3. Provide your address.
4. Register your books.

Note: English-language books only

To order books online:
oreilly.com/store

For questions about products or an order:
orders@oreilly.com

To sign up to get topic-specific email announcements and/or news about upcoming books, conferences, special offers, and new technologies:
elists@oreilly.com

For technical questions about book content:
booktech@oreilly.com

To submit new book proposals to our editors:
proposals@oreilly.com

O'Reilly books are available in multiple DRM-free ebook formats. For more information:
oreilly.com/ebooks

Milton Keynes UK
Ingram Content Group UK Ltd.
UKHW050902210924
448582UK00008B/106